1 MONTH OF
FREE
READING

at
www.ForgottenBooks.com

By purchasing this book you are eligible for one month membership to ForgottenBooks.com, giving you unlimited access to our entire collection of over 1,000,000 titles via our web site and mobile apps.

To claim your free month visit:

www.forgottenbooks.com/free915859

ISBN 978-0-265-95981-7
PIBN 10915859

REPORT

ON THE

SCHOOLS OF NOVA-SCOTIA,

FOR THE YEAR 1851.

BY THE

SUPERINTENDENT OF EDUCATION.

HALIFAX, N. S.:

PRINTED BY RICHARD NUGENT,

PRINTER TO THE HOUSE OF ASSEMBLY,

REPORT.

~~~~~~

Hon. JOSEPH HOWE,
> *Provincial Secretary.*

SIR,—I have now the honor to transmit through you, to His Excellency the Lieutenant-Governor, my second Annual Report on the Schools of Nova Scotia.

I do not think it necessary to enter so largely as in last report, into the details of school instruction and discipline; but shall confine myself to short notices of the following subjects:—

(A) *Report of proceedings, &c.*
  - I. Projects for a Normal School and Assessment.
  - II. Public Meetings, Lectures, &c.
  - III. Associations and Institutes.
  - IV. School Inspection.
  - V. Supply of Books and Apparatus.
  - VI. Changes required in a new School Act.
  - VII. Notices of Commissioners' Districts.
  - VIII. School Libraries.

(B) *Statistical Report*—including remarks on the state of Education, as shown by the tables.

In the Appendix will be found Minutes of Public Meetings—an Address on Free Schools, by Dr. Ryerson—Rules of Associations —Proceedings of Institute at Truro, &c.

(*A*)

REPORT OF PROCEEDINGS, &c.

<hr>

I.   PROJECTS FOR A NORMAL SCHOOL AND ASSESSMENT.

In accordance with the recommendations contained in my Report of last year, I presented to the Committee of the Assembly on Education, sketches of plans for a provincial Training School, and for a county assessment for school purposes.   The former I thought required immediate action—the latter was presented merely to afford opportunity for more mature consideration, in view of the enactment of a new Educational Law, in the present session of the Legislature.

The approbation of the educational committee having been given to the plan for the establishment of a Normal School, a bill for that purpose was introduced into the Legislature by G. R. Young, Esq., chairman of the committee.   Much to my regret, however, and I may add to that of all intelligent persons acquainted with the state of our schools, the bill was lost by a small majority.   I shall not at present make any remarks on the reasons which should have led to an opposite conclusion, as I shall have occasion again to refer to this subject, as well as to the plan for assessment, in a subsequent part of this report.

The Legislature acceded to my request to have a sufficient number of copies of the report printed to furnish every commissioner and teacher with a copy.   Fifteen hundred copies were accordingly printed and distributed, and I trust that the information thus circulated has not been without good effects on the condition of the schools.

II.   PUBLIC MEETINGS AND LECTURES.

The public meetings required by the law, have been held in all the districts.   They were, like those of 1850, not largely but very respectably attended; and I was much cheered by the increased zeal and more enlarged appreciation of the necessity of educational improvement that appeared in most of the counties, as well as by the circumstance that in every case in which resolutions approving of the plans proposed by the Superintendent for a Normal School and Assessment were proposed, they were carried either unanimously or by good majorities.

In addition to addresses at public meetings, I have delivered since the date of last report, sixty-five lectures on education. By means of these lectures, information respecting the means of improvement now in progress has been much more widely diffused than would have been possible had I confined myself to a public meeting for each district; and I have found that these projects for improvement only required to be stated and explained to secure cordial approval.

Under this head I may also mention the publication of a Journal of Education, of which three numbers have been issued at intervals of about two months, and which I trust has served to diffuse a little educational information in localities to which such matter seldom penetrates, and which I have been unable to visit. It has also afforded a useful medium of communication with commissioners and teachers.

The journal of education has been circulated gratis to commissioners and teachers, to the extent of from 2000 to 2500 copies of each number. I trust that the Legislature may afford the means of publishing it monthly in future, and in that case it is probable that a number of paying subscribers might be obtained. I would, however, recommend that commissioners and licensed teachers should continue to receive it gratis. The saving which might be effected by the journal in advertising and other printing, would repay a considerable part of the cost of this gratuitous distribution.

III. ASSOCIATIONS AND INSTITUTES.

In 1850 but one association of teachers existed in the province. Twelve or more are now in operation, and it is the uniform testimony of teachers who are members of them, that they exercise a marked influence on the prosperity of the schools. If such societies were established in every part of the province, this alone would give a most powerful impetus to educational improvement. To further this end, I give in the Appendix the rules of four Associations, for the guidance of teachers who may be disposed to adopt this means of mutual professional instruction.

Encouraged by the success of the Institute held in Pictou in 1850, I have in the past year convened seven similar meetings, in different parts of the province.

An institute of the duration of five days was held in the Horton Academy, by the kind permission of the committee of that institution. It was attended by forty-one teachers, principally from

King's and Hants Counties ; and by the aid of the professors in the academy and college, the Rev. Mr. Somerville and other educationists, the proceedings were rendered highly interesting and instructive. The order of exercises was similar to that of the Pictou institute, described in last report. Lectures were delivered to the institute by Rev. Professor Chipman, Rev. Mr. Somerville, Mr. Randall, and Mr. Willard.

Short institutes of the duration of one day, were held in Yarmouth, Shelburne and Lunenburg, attended respectively by twenty-two, ten and twenty teachers.

An institute of the duration of two days, was held in Sydney, C. B., and was attended by twenty-one teachers. Another of the duration of one day was held in Port Hood, and was attended by fifteen teachers.

In November, an institute of the duration of five days was held in Truro. It was attended by sixty-eight teachers, from the counties of Colchester, Pictou, Halifax, Hants and Cumberland. I had hoped to have had the aid of several literary gentlemen as lecturers at this institute, but was disappointed in almost every instance. Mr. Blanchard, however, the principal of the academy, afforded valuable aid and the institute included several able teachers, some of whom had attended the Pictou institute, and who were prepared to report on the practical operation of suggestions given at that institute, or of methods which they had derived from other sources. I was also able to secure the valuable services of Mr. H. Oldright, as a lecturer on Phonetic Spelling.

Notes of the proceedings of this institute are given in the Appendix.

The principal work of all these institutes has been to explain and illustrate modern and improved methods of instruction and discipline, by lectures and addresses from the Superintendent and others, and by discussions and illustrations of methods, in which the abler and more experienced teachers instruct their less informed brethren, or aid each other in arriving at sound conclusions on the work of their profession. Two hundred and thirty teachers have attended the institutes held in 1850 and '51, all of whom must have received considerable information and much stimulus to advancement in their calling, and to the cultivation of a friendly and profitable intercourse with each other. The following remarks of one of the teachers who attended the institute at Truro, I am sure express the feelings of many others :—

" I have returned with a feeling of delight that those who have minds to appreciate enlightened enterprise, have thought highly of the profession of teaching, and have given their talents to it. One source of regret alone I feel regarding it, and that is, that we continued together for so short a time. When persons come from a distance, the meeting should continue fourteen days, for about the time we were beginning to become acquainted with each other, we had to separate. I feel happier in my work, because many of the plans I have tried in doubt have been tried by others, and that with success; while difficulties with which I have been struggling for years, have been overcome by those who fell upon some simple remedy I never thought of before."

Before leaving this subject, I may remark that the teachers who attend institutes are in general from among the ablest in their respective counties. The numerous incompetent teachers to be found in every district, are too careless or too fearful of contact with their more instructed brethren, to be very desirous of attending either institutes or associations. Hence institutes cannot supply the place of a training school: and on the other hand, regularly trained teachers will be found to be more willing than others to attend institutes or to become members of associations.

Out of the grant of £100 for defraying expenses of institutes, &c., I paid the boarding bills of teachers at Horton, Sydney and Truro. The expenses of the shorter institutes were very trifling. As the teachers who attended at Pictou had no allowance for board, I have presented to each a copy of Norton's Scientific Agriculture, as an aid in teaching Agricultural Chemistry. I have also procured for each of the Teachers' Associations, a copy of the Journal of Education for Upper Canada for one year. Accounts of the expenditures for these purposes accompany this report.

IV. SCHOOL INSPECTION.

During the past year I have visited 260 schools, in all the districts of the Province, and hope, before the expiry of my term of office, to add somewhat to this number, as an illness produced by the fatigues of the Truro institute and subsequent exposure to inclement weather, has prevented me from fulfilling some of my later appointments.

Most of the schools visited in the past year, were such as I had not visited in 1850, as I endeavored to vary my route as much as possible. In their varying degrees of usefulness and respectability, they corresponded very nearly with those visited in 1850. Some were, considering the difficulties under which they laboured, useful and well conducted, others almost worthless. In nearly all, the evils of imperfect school furniture, deficiency of books and apparatus, irregular attendance, want of proper support and encouragement, and defective acquaintance with modern methods of teaching, were to a greater or less degree apparent.

In many of the schools which I had visited in 1850, I was cheered by observing that beneficial changes had been effected. In other instances no improvement was perceptible; and I may observe in general, that in the districts in which education was most defective in 1850, there was the smallest amount of improvement.

I regret that the work of school visitation has necessarily been so imperfectly performed. The field is too wide for one inspector, and can only be properly occupied by a body of local inspectors acting under the superintendent. I believe, however, that the visitation performed has been sufficiently extensive to sow the seed of much good, which may extend into localities not actually visited; and to give clear views of the true nature of the defects of the schools and of the present systems of management.

It cannot be denied that, notwithstanding the present faint signs of incipient elevation, the common school education of this Province is in general far below the wants of the people, and the demands of the age in which they live. A large majority of the schools, as at present taught, supported and attended, are evidently unfit to give the amount of education necessary for the respectable pursuit of any ordinary business, or to extend such education as they can give, to the whole community. As a consequence of this, over large portions of our country, a population is being reared, fitted only to live in poverty and ignorance on its native soil, or to emigrate and furnish drudges to our better educated neighbours, while the rich natural resources of our Province are neglected, or are ruinously wasted by heedless ignorance. Every imperfectly educated country is, in the ordinary recurrence of unfavourable seasons, exposed to famine or to the necessity of emigration, while educated countries are comparatively exempted from such calamities; and I suspect that the present census will evidence an amount of emigration, which, in a young and naturally rich country, must result more from a want of that mental and moral training which enables men to combat the difficulties and improve the advantages of their position, than from any other cause. It is time that the attention of the Legislature were directed to these evils, and that vigorous measures were taken for placing a practically useful education within the reach of all the youth of our country.

V. SUPPLY OF BOOKS AND APPARATUS.

In expending the sum placed at my disposal for this purpose, I have had regard to the same objects which regulated its appropriation in 1850—the supply of existing destitution, and the introduction of superior books and of provincial uniformity.

Arrangements have been made with the Messrs. Chambers, of Edinburgh, by which I have obtained their publications at a reduced price, and have thus been able to supply each district with a larger quantity of books than in 1850. Messrs. Chambers have also promised to supply booksellers here with the educational course, on terms which will enable them to give a discount from the British retail price, to country traders or other wholesale purchasers.

With the view of promoting the study of agricultural chemistry, I contracted with Messrs. Pease & Co., of Albany, the publishers of the American edition of Johnston's catechism, for an edition of 1000 copies, with four pages of useful additional matter compiled by myself. Of these I distributed 600 to the schools, along with 28 dozen of the British edition which I had ordered. The balance of the American edition I disposed of at cost and charges to the booksellers.

In answer to an inquiry respecting Professor Sullivan's " spelling book superseded," which I thought might be useful in enabling some of the teachers to depart from the old spelling book system, the Secretary of the National Board for Ireland has sent a list of prices, the same with those at which the books of the Board are furnished to poor schools in Ireland and to the schools of Canada. On receiving this list, I preferred, instead of sending for the single work which I had desired, to hand over the list to my successor in office, with a recommendation to give it attention in the orders of next year.

There has been some diversity in the modes in which the several Boards of Commissioners have disposed of their shares of the books purchased. I have recommended, when consulted on the subject, to reserve a portion in the hands of the clerk, for sale at cost price, and to distribute the remainder among the schools for the use of poor pupils; giving a larger proportion to poor schools, and requiring that the books should be held as the property of the school, and given to individual scholars only as a loan.

VI. CHANGES REQUIRED IN A NEW SCHOOL ACT.

The subjects treated under this head, are equal in importance to any that can come under the notice of the Legislature; and I trust that the Government and members of the legislative bodies, will enter on their consideration, under the influence of an enlightened regard to the future welfare of the province, rather than under that of the prejudices which may exist in the present.

1. Since the efficacy of any system of instruction must depend on the competency of the teachers employed, means for their training must be provided; and on this account I would strongly insist on the necessity of a provision for the foundation of a *Provincial Normal School.*

The necessity of this, few, I trust, will be disposed to deny. I had scarcely commenced my work of school visitation, when a full conviction of it was produced in my mind. I found that the majority of the teachers were managing their schools on old and obsolete methods, and that they often had a very imperfect acquaintance with the branches which they professed to teach. Lessons in reading, without any explanation or mental training, columns of unintelligible spellings, inability to explain the principles of arithmetic or the elements of English grammar, or to preserve order, except by the harshest and most repulsive methods, formed the rule rather than the exception; and it was not difficult to perceive that a large amount of the public money, as well as of the improvement and future usefulness of the children, was yearly being lost from this cause. Against these evils I have been contending in my lectures, institutes, report and journal, and probably with some success; but the experience of every country which has attempted to educate its people, teaches us that there is no effectual remedy other than providing teachers with a sound and practical preliminary training.

One efficient Normal School is better than several of inferior capabilities. Hence the State of New York and Upper Canada have, profiting by the experience of other parts of America, each established but one Normal School. One school would consequently be amply sufficient for Nova Scotia.

It should, if possible, be situated in a rural district, because there alone can the important requisites of cheap board and efficient control on the part of the principal be secured.

The principal should be the Provincial Superintendent of Education, whose duties, (exclusive of school inspection) he could perform, and teach some of the higher classes in the Normal School. He should have two assistants, who should be teachers of first rate qualifications, and selected by the principal.

Instruction should be free to persons having a common school education, and pledging themselves to become teachers within the Province; and the benefits of the school should be made accessible to pupils from all the counties, by giving to each Board of Commissioners power to send a number of pupils proportioned to population and to pay, if necessary, the travelling expenses of poor pupils.

The course of instruction should be limited to common school branches, and those collateral to them, with the addition of elementary and practical mathematics; and power should be given to the principal to send a limited number of graduates of the school, desiring to qualify themselves for grammar schools, as free scholars to academies and colleges receiving provincial aid.

The terms of study, examinations, &c., could not be better

arranged than in imitation of those of Upper Canada and New York; but much of these arrangements should be left to the discretion of the principal.

The cost of such institution, on the lowest scale consistent with extensive usefulness, would be £900 for buildings, furniture and site, and £700 per annum for salaries and incidental expenses.

2. The second requisite for a really useful and progressive law, is provision for *free schools*, supported, in addition to the provincial grant, at least in part by an equitable rate on the property of all, instead of the present very defective method of fees per scholar.

Our present law, by providing a provincial grant, acknowledges that education is a benefit to all interests, public as well as private; but by requiring or permitting the parent to pay fees for the education of each child, it practically narrows the benefit of really useful instruction to a small part of the population, and requires the majority of the children to put up with a mere fraction of that training, which it is the interest and duty of their country to provide for them in full measure. Between that class which can give its children a thorough common school education on the present plan, and that which is willing to send its children to school as pauper or free scholars, there is a still larger class excluded from the school by poverty or carelessness, or receiving only a very small share of its benefits. I can find for this great evil no other remedy than that of adopting the method of general and in part compulsory assessment, which has so extensively benefitted the New England States, and has been introduced into Canada so successfully, that the chief superintendent of Upper Canada testifies, that free schools have increased the number of pupils by 50 per cent. in some cases, and in others by 300 per cent.

This mode of supporting schools has long been before the people of Nova Scotia, and in the last two years it has been very extensively discussed throughout the province; and I think I may add, without fear of contradiction, approved by the majority in every instance in which it has been properly explained. It has been approved by resolutions passed at 15 of the public meetings held in the past year, and these the largest of the meetings held; and in several other meetings where no resolutions were offered, the expressed opinions were in its favour. It is now, I believe, understood and approved by the more intelligent supporters of schools throughout the province.

I had the honor last winter to propose to the Legislature a plan for Assessment for Schools, which has been explained in all the public meetings of the past year. To this plan I still adhere. It is substantially the same with the system adopted and successfully working in Upper Canada. In that province, since 1841, each county has been required to raise by assessment a sum equal to the provincial grant. These two sums form a part of the salaries of teachers, and the remainder is raised in the separate districts or sections by rate-bills, subscription or assessment, voluntarily determined at a meeting called for that purpose by the trustees.

I would desire to improve on the Canadian system only in one particular. In Canada the taxation of the county does not necessarily ensure a free school, since the meeting of each district may, if it think proper, collect the teacher's salary by rate-bill per scholar. In this country, taxation to any amount, however small, must be accompanied by such arrangements as will cause the trustees to establish free schools.

On this plan the school would be supported by the provincial grant, a like sum from the county, and a third sum raised, to any amount agreed on by the trustees and people, either by district assessment or by subscription, not per scholar, but to form a fund for supporting a free school. I may mention that this last kind of subscription is now in use in some districts, and has worked well. Each inhabitant is called on for a subscription, according to his means or inclination, and allowed to send as many children to school as he pleases. This, though inferior to assessment as being less equitable, secures a free school.

This three-fold method of support commends itself on the following grounds :—1. The province contributes because the benefit is national. 2. The county contributes because the wealthier parts of counties are interested in the prosperity of the poorer portions. 3. The district contributes that it may feel a direct interest in its own school, and that facilities may be afforded for the payment of part of the teacher's salary in produce where necessary. 4. This method has been successful in another province not very dissimilar from Nova Scotia in its circumstances. 5. It is approved by the highest educational authorities, and is embodied in the laws of most countries which support schools by assessment. Lastly. Without enforcing a heavy tax, it will relieve the burdens of parents in poor districts, improve the salaries of teachers, and give free schools to all. It will thus afford most of the benefits of a complete compulsory assessment, without being so objectionable, and may in a short time cause the whole support of the schools, to be raised by assessment.

In the Appendix will be found an address by the Rev. E. Ryerson, D.D., in which the argument for assessment is well stated.

3. *The Superintendent of Education*, being Principal of the Normal School, should be released from the work of school inspection, and give instructions at the Normal School instead. He should be authorized to publish annually a sufficient number of copies of the School Law, accompanied by the forms required and by short instructions, to supply all the commissioners, teachers and

trustees with copies. This is absolutely necessary, especially to the proper performance of the duties of trustees, and has been too long neglected. He should also be empowered to issue a cheap Educational newspaper. £100 per annum would suffice for these objects.

4. The duties of *School Commissioners* and their *Clerk* should be more definitely fixed, without however encroaching on a proper degree of freedom of action. This is rendered necessary by the circumstance that the vagueness of the law has led to much uncertainty and defectiveness in the management of the affairs of some of the districts. In this matter the procedure of those Boards which have been most successful may be taken as a guide.

The commissioners should have power to arbitrate and decide in cases where the trustees refuse to sign the school returns, or where disputes arise between trustees and teachers.

The commissioners should also be empowered to spend a part of the sum allowed by law to be given to poor districts, in hiring itinerant teachers for thinly settled and poor places unable to support permanent schools ; and in districts where it is impossible to establish Grammar Schools, the Board should be allowed to draw from the Treasury the grammar school grant for the purpose of employing such itinerant teachers if required. I attach much importance to these provisions, since in some parts of the province there are many poor settlements unable to maintain schools, and since some of the counties, which have many such poor settlements, have under the present act been unable to draw their grammar school grants.

5. The *religious element* in common school education is recognized in our law, as in that of Canada, by the appointment of all clergymen and ministers of religion to be school visitors. They are thus invited to visit schools at any time, to give suggestions, and to inquire into their progress and discipline.

Teachers should be enjoined to inculcate respect to religion in general, and to teach by precept and example the principles of christian morality as the basis of future good and orderly conduct, but to give no instruction of a denominational character except by request of the parents.

6. *School Inspection* is of great service in stimulating teachers, trustees and people, and in collecting educational information. It is best effected by local officers, acting under a superintendent, furnished with forms by him, and reporting regularly. Some suitable person of respectable acquirements and education could readily be found to accept such an office in any of the districts. Wherever practicable, the school inspector should be the clerk of the commissioners. An annual inspection of all the schools could in this way be effected for about £250.

7. The proper performance of the duties of *Trustees* is essential to the useful working of any system of public instruction in a free country. Hitherto, however, these duties have not been faithfully and intelligently performed in one fourth of the sections.

The trustees are properly the people's representatives in school affairs. Provision should therefore be made for their due and orderly election, for the retirement of one member of the Board annually and the election of another, and for the systematic management of the affairs of the school.

The trustees should be required, immediately on their election, to appoint one of themselves or some other person to be their Secretary, who should keep their records and accounts, and collect subscriptions and assessments. They should call an annual meeting to elect a new trustee in place of the retiring one, and to receive their report and estimate of necessary expenses for the ensuing year; and the time of this meeting should be fixed by law. The meeting called for these purposes should, in event of county assessment being introduced, have the power of deciding in what manner the part of the support of the school to be raised in the district shall be collected—whether by subscription or assessment; and the secretary of the trustees should have a commission for collecting such sums. Another duty of the trustees is to engage a teacher who must have been previously licensed, and by such arrangements as those above suggested, they should have powers which may enable them safely to make and certainly to fulfil such engagements. Provisions for all these purposes are embraced in the School Law of Upper Canada, and it is to be hoped that by introducing them here, this weak point of our school system may be effectually strengthened.

The trustees should also be limited in their power of establishing too great a number of schools. Districts should be as large as they can conveniently be made, in order that they may be able to support efficient schools. Various local interests, however, tend to set up within the district several small schools of a low character. To prevent this, the trustees should be allowed to recognize within their district only one school for each fifty persons between five and sixteen; and when new school houses are erected, they should be required to place them in the geographical centres of the districts, unless authorized to do otherwise by a regularly called public meeting. "We require," says the last Massachusetts Report, "large houses, large teachers, long schools, and in order to this there must be large districts;" and Dr. Ryerson asserts in his report for 1850, that "it is a fact established by a large investigation of facts, that pupils residing at the greatest distance from the school they attend, make on an average the greatest improvement."

8. The *Trustees of Towns and Villages* should be appointed by the people, at annual meetings, as in the country districts, and there should be but one Board for each town. They should, as in the country, be required to present to the annual meeting an estimate of the expense of the schools, and thus to establish free schools regularly graded into primary, common and high, for all the children.

Such arrangements are especially necessary in the towns and villages, since in these the affairs of the schools have often been managed with much less system than in the country, and the education given has, when the importance and means of the places are considered, been lamentably defective.

9. The present law is unsuited to the circumstances of the city of Halifax; and if the commissioners should not succeed in carrying into effect their excellent scheme of ward schools and city assessment, the city might be brought under the operation of the act in the following manner:—Each ward to elect three trustees, having especial jurisdiction in their own ward, the whole trustees unitedly forming a City School Committee, with powers similar to those of the country trustees. The city would then receive its share of the county assessment, and could contribute by local assessment or subscription, the additional sums required, according to estimates furnished by the school committee.

The total additional expense of the improvements above suggested, will be about £800 annually. This covers the cost of district inspection, normal school, travelling expenses of normal school students, supply of copies of acts and instructions, and educational journal. My observation of the state of schools in this Province, and the information which I have collected respecting those of other countries, justify me in asserting that the saving effected in the school grant, without taking into account any higher considerations, would render the expenditure of such a sum in these ways, highly economical.

For additional facts bearing on this subject, I beg to refer to the Statistical Report, and to the view of the state of education given in my report of last year.

VII. NOTICES OF COMMISSIONERS' DISTRICTS.

1. *King's County.*

On the day following the close of the institute at Horton, the public meeting for this county was held in Kentville. It was well attended, and resolutions were passed unanimously in favor of the plans for a Normal School and assessment. I lectured to good audiences at Kentville, Western Cornwallis, Black Rock and Aylesford. I visited eight schools, most of them in an improving condition. I trust that the institute of last spring will produce beneficial effects of a marked character.

2. *Annapolis.*

The public meeting was held at Bridgetown, and was well at-attended. Resolutions in favor of the Normal School and assessment were passed unanimously. I lectured at Bridgetown, Annapolis and Caledonia.

I visited fifteen schools in this district, several of them in a very efficient state. Much improvement has been made in the Annapolis academy, but the county has sustained a considerable loss in the removal of Mr. Hart from Paradise. I regret that a miscalculation as to time prevented me from reaching some places, especially in the southern part of the county and on the Bay shore, which I had intended to visit.

Rev. Mr. Robertson of Bridgetown informed me that, with the aid of the apparatus furnished to the board of commissioners, he had delivered a course of lectures on agricultural chemistry, and proposed repeating the course in another part of the county. I have no doubt that these lectures will be of much service, and may cause the subject to be introduced into some of the schools.

In their report, the commissioners for this county represent the necessity of giving to the board the power of decision in the case of trustees refusing to sign school returns, and thus depriving the teacher of his share of the provincial grant, without sufficient cause. I have already referred to this subject.

They also object to the restriction laid upon them in Schedule B of the present Act, by which they are required to establish Grammar Schools in Annapolis, Bridgetown, Paradise and Nictaux, to the exclusion of all other districts. On this subject they remark :

" In the first place this arrangement appears to be tantamount to an absolute exclusion of all interference on the part of the Board with this part of the educational grant to the county. It appears moreover to savour of invidious distinction, for on reference to the Schedule just quoted, it will be discovered that Annapolis County is the only county in the province that has been subject to such close restriction. * * * Through the practical working of the legal apportionment of which we complain, this county has been deprived of one-half its grant for Academies, (Grammar Schools,) during the current half year."

I concur with the commissioners in objecting to restrictions of this kind. The *number* of grammar schools should be fixed, but their localities should be determined by the amount of effort which districts desirous of such schools may put forth.

3. *Digby.*

The meeting at Digby was small, owing to wet weather. The persons present, however, manifested an excellent spirit in reference to educational improvement, and resolutions in favour of a Training School and of Assessment were passed unanimously. I lectured to good audiences at Digby, Sand Cove and Westport.

I visited ten schools, some of them of low character. At Digby, Bear River, Weymouth and Westport, however, very good schools have been established.

4. *Clare.*

Having been detained two days in Westport by stormy weather which prevented me from crossing St. Mary's Bay, I arrived at the Town-house nearly an hour after the time appointed for my meeting, and was somewhat surprised to find a large number of persons assembled,—my former meeting having been small. I soon learned, however, that a considerable number of the persons present had been collected by agitators against the principle of assessment. No resolutions were offered, but an excellent opportunity was afforded of explaining the true nature of the measures proposed.

I visited fifteen schools. The general character of education in this district is low, owing to the difficulty of procuring teachers having a sufficient knowledge of the French and English languages, and to the practice of setting up too many small schools in each district. There are, however, a few really good teachers; and I was much pleased by hearing that some of the young female teachers had, since my last visit, been exerting themselves to improve their acquaintance with the English branches. The establishment of a Normal School would be of especial service to districts like Clare.

5. *Yarmouth.*

The meeting in Yarmouth was well attended, and a resolution in favour of a Normal School was passed unanimously. The principle of Assessment was, however, vigorously opposed, and a resolution in its favour was passed by a majority of 34 to 17, in a meeting of about 120 persons. In this county, indeed, I have found a more active opposition to School Assessment than in any other in the province. I lectured to good audiences at Beaver River, Yarmouth and Carlton.

The Academy at Yarmouth was in good working order, and an excellent school, fitted up with improved furniture, blackboards, &c., and taught on the plans of the Massachusetts schools, had been established at Milton. I visited only nine schools.

6. *Argyle.*

The meeting at Tusket was small, and no resolutions were offered, though several gentlemen present spoke in approval of the plans proposed in my address. Two gentlemen from the neighboring district of Yarmouth, emulating the " Eteignoirs" or extinguishers of Lower Canada, attended this meeting, with the express purpose of opposing Free Schools and Assessment. I advertised a lecture for Argyle, but could not collect an audience. I saw but four schools in operation, many of the districts being vacant. The school house at Tusket had been newly fitted up, and was under a good teacher ; and the other schools which I visited were of creditable character. It is evident, however, that there is still very great destitution of education in many parts of this township.

7. *Barrington.*

The meeting at Barrington was small, but the discussion was interesting and animated. Resolutions were passed approving of Assessment and of the appointment of a Superintendent. I lectured in the evening to a good audience, and a resolution was moved and passed unanimously in favour of a Normal School. I also lectured at Port LaTour, and had advertised a lecture for Cape Sable Island, but was prevented by illness and stormy weather.

I visited seven schools, most of them in creditable condition. The female teachers of Barrington are especially deserving of credit for their knowledge of the branches required in their schools and of improved methods of teaching. The coloured School of Port LaTour is deserving of notice, as one of the best of its class in the rural districts. The children appear intelligent ; and I was informed that the parents, though poor, contribute ten pounds per annum toward the salary of the teacher.

8. *Shelburne.*

The meeting at Shelburne was very small, and no resolutions were proposed. An evening lecture, however, was well attended. There appears to prevail in this township an indifference to the subject of education, which contrasts unfavourably with the comparative activity in Barrington. I visited but six schools. One of the teachers in the town of Shelburne had, since my last visit, fitted up his school with improved furniture at his own expense.

9. *Queen's County.*

The meeting in Liverpool was small, owing in part to its having been inadvertently appointed for Whit Monday. No resolutions were moved, but it seemed to be the understanding that the persons present adhered to the resolutions of last year. I lectured to good audiences at Liverpool, Caledonia and Port Medway.

I visited fourteen schools of various character. The Academy at Liverpool at the time of my visit was a combined Grammar and Common School, with two teachers. The Grammar School at Port Medway was in efficient condition. It has a good building, furnished with stools for separate scholars, and long desks, as in some of the New York schools.

10. *Lunenburg.*

The meeting for this county was well attended, and the discussion was of an animated character. Resolutions were passed in favour of general assessment, and of a Normal School; the latter unanimously. I lectured in Lunenburg, Mahone Bay and Chester,—in the two former places to good audiences.

I visited 13 schools, some of them of high character, others comparatively inefficient.

At a meeting held in February, the Board of Commissioners passed the following resolution, with one dissentient: " Resolved, that this Board approves of the principle of taxation for the support of Schools."

11. *City of Halifax.*

The meeting for Halifax was very small, and contented itself with passing a resolution requesting the Commissioners to proceed with the agitation of their plan for city assessment. On this subject the Commissioners remark in their last report:

" In pursuance of the duty devolving on the Commissioners, and in accordance with their report of last year, they prepared, and early in the present year, published an abstract of a " Scheme for bringing about a better regulated and more uniform system of education in the city, by means of assessment."

" They laid the subject before his worship the Mayor and City Council, and specially invited them to attend the educational meeting on Thursday, the 12th of June, at which J. W. Dawson, Esquire, Superintendent of Education presided. In consequence of the non-attendance of the city authorities at the said meeting, it was moved by the hon. W. Young, and resolved "that the Mayor be requested to call a public meeting on the following Tuesday, for the purpose of considering whether an assessment of the city should be made for the support of schools."

" Various occurrences have prevented the Commissioners from carrying out the above resolution. They are, however, still anxious for their fellow-citizens to see the advantages to be derived from that mode of supporting and managing schools, and purpose holding a meeting at some early period for diffusing information on the subject."

" Education in Halifax remains in about the same condition as when the Commissioners presented their report to your Excellency, at the close of last year. The want of a general system and uniformity of mode, are serious disadvantages to both teachers and children, and account for much of the existing deficiency."

The city of Halifax contributed last year for the support of its public schools, a sum only equal to its provincial grant—thus placing itself in this respect below the level of the poorest country districts. When we add to this, that there is no gradation of schools, and no public school committee, or trustees representing the people, it is not difficult to appreciate the grounds for the complaints of the commissioners.

12. *Western District of Halifax.*

The meeting for this district was held in Dartmouth. It was slenderly attended, and no resolutions were offered, though some excellent remarks were made by gentlemen present. I visited only four of the schools of this district, but may perhaps be able to see others in the course of the winter. The commissioners thus conclude their report on the state of the schools:—

·" The commissioners in closing this their second report to your Excellency, feel gratified that their exertions in the cause of education have been productive of some good. Since their appointment by your Excellency, they have had several examinations of the teachers, and they have witnessed with pleasure the improvements which have from time to time been made by many of them, in several of the branches of their profession. The books and maps which the commissioners have been enabled to distribute among the several districts, will, in the opinion of the Board, do much to raise the standard of education, and will no doubt induce the inhabitants of each district to extend their efforts for the support of the schools."

13. *Eastern District of Halifax.*

The meeting for this district was not large, but much interest was expressed in its objects. A resolution was passed expressing regret that the Normal School bill of last session had failed, and another inviting the attention of teachers to the advantages of institutes. I lectured to good audiences at Upper Musquodoboit and Musquodoboit Harbour.

I visited nine schools in this district, some of them taught by excellent and improving teachers, and two of them fitted with new furniture,—on the New England plan. The following extracts from the Report of the Commissioners expose some startling facts respecting the condition of the shore districts :

"Several members of the Board from personal inspection, and other means of information, report, that the settlements along the coast from Musquodoboit Harbour, eastward, to Sheet Harbour, with few exceptions, are without any means of education whatever, and even the schools in operation, with one or two exceptions, are in a very inefficient state.

For example, in Petpiswick, containing thirty families, there has been no regular school since the commencement of the settlement. The same thing is true of Abbecumbec, Clam Harbour, and Little Harbour, with twenty-five families. A similar example is that of Owl's Head, and the west side of the entrance of Ship Harbour, with sixteen families,—of the east side of the entrance of Ship Harbour, with fourteen families,—of Shoal Bay, with thirteen families,—of Tangier, with twenty families ; and the east side of Spry Harbour, including Taylor's Head, with twenty families.

Thus within these settlements, there are one hundred and thirty-eight families, who have never had any regular means of education whatever.

At the entrance of Musquodoboit Harbor, with twenty families, and both sides of the Head of Jeddore, with twenty families, there have been no schools for the last year, while, from Sheet Harbour, eastward to the county line, there is a similar lamentable deficiency.

In the Middle and Upper Settlement of Musquodoboit, during the past year, the schools in the several localities have, with few exceptions, been in operation ; but only a small minority can be regarded as efficient, in consequence of the low rate of remuneration on the part of the people, and the meagre qualifications of the teachers— still, the Board believe, that the interest of the community in the cause of education is increasing, and the desire for a better class of teachers is manifest in the fact, that advertisements for superior teachers for several schools have appeared in the newspapers.

It is a matter of regret that a considerable number of schools will be vacant during the winter ; and there is little doubt that the number of qualified teachers is lessening, and should this state of things continue, the cause of education will suffer materially.

To remedy these evils the Board earnestly recommend the speedy establishment of the proposed Normal School, as also the adoption of the principle of assessment for the support of education. Whether the assessment should meet the whole expense, or whether it should be in conjunction with the present governmental allowance and fees from the pupils, may be a matter of opinion, and ought to be the subject of grave discussion; but as to the principle itself the Board are unanimous that it ought to be adopted as soon as convenient."

It is to be hoped that, under a new law, the commissioners will be enabled to employ, at least, temporary teachers in the destitute districts above referred to.

14. *St. Mary's.*

The meeting for this district was respectable, and resolutions were passed in favour of a Normal School and assessment. I lectured at Sherbrooke and at the Backlands, to good audiences.

I visited eight schools in this district—three of which were of respectable character. In this district, as in Eastern Halifax, temporary teachers for shore districts, might be usefully employed.

15. *Eastern District of Guysboro'.*

The meeting in Guysboro' was respectable, though not large, and much interest was expressed in its objects. Resolutions in favour of a Normal School and of assessment were passed—the former unanimously. I lectured to good audiences at Guysboro'. and Cape Canseau.

I visited 16 schools in this district, four or five of which, including the Grammar Schools at Guysboro'. and Cape Canseau, were in efficient condition. The grammar school house at Cape Canseau is the best school building in the district. Many parts of the south shore of Guysboro'. are very destitute of schools, and might be benefitted by the employment of itinerant teachers.

16. *County of Sydney.*

The meeting in Antigonish was small. A resolution was passed in favour of a Normal School. I lectured in the evening to a good audience.

I visited 13 schools—five of which were of respectable character. I found the village of Antigonish still destitute of a public school house.

17. *Richmond.*

The meeting at Arichat, though not large, was of an influentia, and respectable character. Resolutions in favour of Assessmentl a Normal School, and the erection of better school buildings and better support of schools, were passed unanimously. I lectured to a good audience at Arichat, and to a few persons at Grand River.

I visited thirteen schools, four of which were in efficient condition. The schools of this district are on the whole poorly supported, and not sufficiently provided with the necessary means of instruction.

18. *Cape Breton and Victoria.*

The meeting at Sydney was not largely attended; a number of leading and influential persons, however, were present. A resolution in favour of Assessment was adopted. I lectured at Sydney and North Sydney, to good audiences; and to thin meetings at Boulardarie and Bedeque.

I visited fourteen schools, six of them in an efficient state. Two good teachers had, since my last visit, been established in Sydney, one of them a graduate of the Edinburgh Normal School. Mr. Monro's school at Boulardarie Island still continues to be of great service in training teachers, and well illustrates the fact that a good teacher can secure a large school even in the most secluded and scattered districts.

It would be well to insert in the Schedule of grammar school monies, a provision enabling the commissioners, in event of part of their share of that fund being unappropriated, to aid poor pupils intending to be teachers, in attending the schools of Mr. Monro of Boulardarie, or Mr. McKay of Sydney, with a limited portion of the grant.

19. *Northern Inverness.*

The meeting at the Forks of Margaree River was very thinly attended, and no resolutions were offered. I visited five schools. Two of these were in good working condition. Mr. Ayre was still persevering in the attempt to establish a Grammar School at the mouth of Margaree, but had met with many difficulties.

20. *Southern Inverness.*

The meeting at Port Hood was slenderly attended, and no resolutions were offered. I visited eight schools, two of which were of very respectable character. No Grammar School had been established in this district.

21. *Stirling.*

The meeting at Tatamagouche was small. Resolutions were, however, passed in favour of a Normal School and Assessment. I lectured at New Annan, and visited five schools, most of them of respectable character.

22. *Cumberland.*

The meeting in Amherst was well attended. Resolutions in favour of a Normal School and Assessment were adopted unanimously. I lectured at Amherst, Minudie and Pugwash.

I visited twelve schools, six of which were in efficient condition. Considerable signs of improvement were visible since my last visit. A school recently established in Amherst had adopted the new furniture. A neat and well planned building was in course of erection in Wallace ; and Mr. Seaman, of Minudie, was building at his own cost an excellent school house for that village.

The Amherst Female Seminary had undergone extensive improvements since last year. It has now a large and well planned building, six teachers, 24 boarders from various parts of the province, and 8 day scholars; and has been attended in the past year by 3 free pupils, qualifying themselves to be teachers. I mention these details, because the institution is not noticed in the tables, and has received a small grant; to which it certainly has a claim on the same ground with the Academies for the higher education of young men.

23. *Parrsboro'.*

The meeting for this district was small. Resolutions were, however, passed in favour of assessment, and a training school. I advertised a lecture for Advocate Harbour, but a violent storm prevented an audience from assembling, and I had to content myself with addressing a few persons who assembled on the following morning.

I visited five schools. Some of them are taught by respectable teachers—but most appear to be poorly supported.

24. *Colchester—(Southern District.)*

The meeting in Truro was small, owing to wet weather, and no resolutions were offered. I lectured at Truro and Five Islands, and visited 10 schools, most of them taught by competent teachers. A resolution in favour of assessment was passed at the meeting at Five Islands.

25. *Western Hants.*

No resolutions were offered at the meeting in Windsor, though much interest in the subject was expressed by several speakers. I lectured to good audiences in Windsor and Walton.

I visited 8 schools in this district; three of them in an efficient state.

26. *Eastern Hants.*

The meeting for this district was well attended, though the day was wet; and resolutions were passed in favor of a Normal School and assessment. I lectured to a small audience at Shubenacadie.

I visited 10 schools in this district, in which education has evidently been advancing, though some difficulty is still experienced in securing competent teachers for the poorer districts. Three of the schools have been fitted up with the new furniture.

27. *Northern Pictou.*

The meeting for this district was very small, and no resolutions were offered. A general agreement with the measures proposed was, however, expressed. At an evening lecture in the town of Pictou, which was very largely and respectably attended, resolutions in favour of a training school and assessment were passed unanimously.

I was prevented by illness from visiting schools in November as I had intended, I hope however, toward the close of winter, to make up for this deficiency. The grammar schools of this district are in efficient condition, and I am aware that much improvement has been made in the common schools. The Academy and Infant School also continue to maintain their former efficiency.

At a meeting held in February, the following resolution was unanimously adopted by the Commissioners :

" That in the opinion of this Board, the principle of assessment and the establishment of a Normal School, as recommended by the Superintendent of education, are admirably adapted to meet the exigencies of this Province ; and the Commissioners would respectfully but urgently recommend the adoption of these improvements, in any future legislation affecting the educational interests of the Province."

28. *Southern Pictou.*

The meeting for this district was respectable, and much interest was expressed on the subject. Resolutions in favour of assessment and a Normal School, and providing for the circulation of petitions in their favour, were passed unanimously.

I visited ten schools in this district, most of them of respectable character. It has two good grammar schools, and two of the common schools have been fitted with good furniture.

———

As a general summary of facts under this head, I may mention that at all the meetings, and in a more summary manner in all the evening lectures, I have explained the plans for assessment, a Normal School and better organization of the affairs of the districts already referred to. At 15 public meetings resolutions were passed in favour of county assessment, and at 16 resolutions were passed in favour of a Normal School. In several other meetings, and at many of the evening lectures, the expression of opinion was entirely in favour of these measures. In favour of a Normal School and of better regulation of the duties of trustees, the opinion seems to be nearly universal.

For statistical information on the several districts, I beg leave to refer to the Tables.

VIII. SCHOOL LIBRARIES.

The School Libraries purchased with the grants for 1850 and '51, were not ready for distribution until the autumn of last year. The Superintendent having undertaken the task of their distribution, allotted them as nearly as possible in accordance with the population of the districts, and made arrangements for having them forwarded. Intimation has already been received that most of the parcels have reached their destinations; a few cases, however, at the date of writing this Report, still remain in Halifax, no conveyance for them having been found.

Rules were prepared, on the plan of allowing each school to have as far as possible a share of the books, on loan, for a limited period; and having been approved by the Governor in Council, were printed and distributed.

There seems no reason to doubt that these libraries will powerfully tend to cultivate a taste for useful reading among the young people of the Province, and thereby elevate the tone of public intelligence and morals. Should the grant be continued, in a few years each school will have the privilege of receiving annually a supply of books, sufficient to allow all its more advanced pupils and their parents constantly to participate in the benefits of the library.

CONCLUDING REMARKS.

THE nature of the duties of my office, and its limited powers, as well as the state of the schools, have required me to act rather as an educational missionary than in a merely official capacity. I have been obliged to select from the multitude of useful employments inviting attention, those which seemed most urgent, and not only to promote the successful working of the present law, but to prepare the public mind for a new and improved educational system.

I have experienced many of the difficulties which attend the agitation of new and untried plans, and also of those which result from the want of enlightened public spirit, unhappily too prevalent in this Province, especially in those places in which the benefits of education have been but little diffused. I must, however, testify that I have found the majority of the commissioners, trustees and teachers, as well as a large proportion of the people, desirous of progress and of information as to the best means of securing it. I may add, without arrogating any peculiar merit to myself, that the appointment of a Superintendent and the operation of the present law, have extensively stirred the public mind on the subject of Education, and prepared it to a considerable extent for improved modes of conducting and supporting schools.

A great duty now devolves on the Government and Legislature. A good school law, fitted for permanent use yet progressive in its tendency, and providing for an orderly, systematic and efficient management of the schools, would be one of the greatest blessings that legislation could confer on this country. In the preceding pages I have endeavored to show, that to effect this great result it will not be necessary to discard our present law, but merely to engraft on it certain new provisions already approved by experience abroad.

Every inhabitant of a free country should have sufficient mental training to enable him to conduct an ordinary business, and to inform himself respecting the improvements in his occupation—the laws and institutions of his country—the duties that devolve on him in private life or in public offices to which he may be called, and his higher moral and religious duties and interests; as well as to dispose him to avoid the errors, deceptions and vices to which uncultivated minds are peculiarly liable. These should be the aims of public elementary instruction, and nothing less should satisfy those whose province it is to frame the laws by which it shall be regulated and promoted.

In conclusion, I beg leave to express my obligations to His Excellency and the members of the Government, as well as to gentlemen of all denominations and parties throughout the Province with whom I have been brought into contact in the discharge of the duties of my office, for the kindness and co-operation which I have experienced ; and my hope that the labours of the past two years, however imperfect, may form the introduction to brighter pages in the Educational History of our Province.

I have the honour to be,
Your obedient servant,

JOHN WILLIAM DAWSON.

JANUARY 29th, 1852.

(B)

STATISTICAL REPORT.

REMARKS ON THE TABLES.

The statistical tables of the past year are much more complete than those of 1850. There are, however, still some deficiencies, and it is to be feared that the registers of daily attendance are yet very imperfectly kept in many of the schools.

I have endeavoured to obtain for the present report a statement of the total number of sections in each district, with the view of estimating the number of vacant sections. There are, however, many blanks in this column ; and there is reason to fear that in several districts the division into sections has been very imperfect, and that no permanent numbers have been attached to them; though this is necessary to enable trustees to exercise their functions as a corporation.

It would appear that in some districts there are a number of vacant sections; while in others the number of schools exceeds that of sections.

Colchester, St. Mary's, and Northern Inverness, furnish examples of the first of these conditions, and Lunenburg and Digby of the second. It is very probable that in some of the districts these differences may result from the formation of too small sections, unable to support schools, or from the establishment of too many schools in a section. There can be no question however, that the poorer sections in many of the districts have been, during the last two years, in a very destitute condition, and that special provisions under the new law are required for their relief.

The support of schools shows no improvement worthy of notice, the sum raised for £1 of provincial grant, being in 1851 £2 4 7, and in 1850 £2 4 3. In some of the districts, however, there appears to have been a falling off, and in others a corresponding increase. It will be observed that the sum raised in proportion to the provincial grant varies very much in the several districts. Halifax, Lunenburg and Richmond, contribute the lowest sums. Southern Colchester, Cumberland and Southern Pictou, the largest.

Table 2, shows a small increase in the number of pupils. It is deserving of attention that the number of female pupils is smaller than that of males, especially in some of the eastern districts; and making every allowance for the earlier age at which girls leave school, there is reason to fear that in many places their education has been much neglected.

From the imperfect returns of the number of children between 4 and 15, it would appear that about 20,000 children have received no benefit from our school system during the past year, and it is a striking fact that, notwithstanding this deficiency of education. only from 4 to 5 free scholars on the average attend each school, although 8 are allowed by law. It must also be remarked that there are at present no means of ascertaining the number of pupils destitute of education, in those poor and scattered settlements which have no regular schools. General assessment affords the only remedy for these evils.

The averages shown in Table 3, present the facts above referred to in a very striking light. The average attendance, which represents the real amount of instruction, is only 20½ for each school. The number in occasional attendance, or whole number on the list, is 30 & 7-tenths; while the average number of children per section is no less than 58 & 7-tenths. It thus appears that less than one half of the children of the province are in the actual enjoyment of the benefits of such education as our common schools are capable of giving.

From the columns showing the sex of teachers, it is apparent that the practice of changing teachers in the winter and summer schools is very prevalent. This is a serious evil, and exists to a greater extent in the western than in the eastern districts. A good teacher, whether male or female, should be retained, where practicable, during the whole year, otherwise the support of the profession must be too precarious to attract competent persons.

The average salaries of teachers are a little higher than last year, partly in consequence of a larger number of grammar schools being established. When it is considered that the teacher's salary includes his board, and that under the present defective systems of management, it is often collected with difficulty, it must be confessed that the average remuneration is far below the requirements of a good system of public instruction. Both the certainty and amount of the teacher's salary would be improved by a county assessment, and by more perfect arrangements for the performance of the duties of trustees.

It appears that during the past year, the number of schools, not teaching grammar and geography, has somewhat diminished. The school apparatus has increased considerably, though there is still a lamentable deficiency, and it is much to be feared that the want of such apparatus as wall maps and black boards, indicates a corresponding deficiency in the support and management of the schools.

Several schools have introduced the important improvement of registers of errors and merits, and a few have been fitted up with new and improved furniture. Other schools, beside those noticed in the table, have been improved in their furniture; and I have reason to believe that all the new school houses now being erected, will be better planned than the old buildings. There is still a very general and lamentable deficiency in the school buildings, in respect of comfortable and suitable furniture, adequate dimensions, out-houses and play grounds.

The number of grammar schools has increased in the past year, and eleven of them have introduced the study of agricultural chemistry, which is also taught in some of the common schools. There is still great difficulty in many districts in obtaining the required number of pupils in the higher branches; and there can be no doubt that, considered as institutions for supplying a higher education than that of the common schools, the grammar schools are in general very defective. It must be admitted, however, that some of them have, in the past year, attained a very high degree of usefulness.

On the whole, the returns of the past year indicate progress, but at no very rapid rate.

The destitution of education, low character of schools, and small remuneration of teachers, are evils of appalling magnitude, amounting to the want of at least one half of that amount of mental and moral culture which the youth of our country should receive in public schools. Should a Normal School and assessment be provided for in a new law, I have no doubt that the reports of the next few years will show rapid changes for the better. Without such provisions, all the exertions of the Superintendent and Commissioners will be able to secure only very slow and limited improvement.

NOTE.—The Returns from Cape Breton and Victoria, have not yet been received.—Feb. 18.

TABLE I. *Schools in operation—Number of Districts—Support of Schools.*

DISTRICT.	No. of Schools.		Number of Districts	Support from People.									Support from Province.									Amt. from people for £1 from province.		
	Winter.	Summer		Winter.			Summer.			Total.			Winter.			Summer.			Total.					
City of Halifax,	14	14	14	366	8	11	321	6	3	687	15	2	335			350	—	—	685	—	—	1	—	1½
Eastern Halifax,	26	27	32	402	13	—	309	14	6	712	7	6	202	1	5	199	15	3½	401	16	8½	1	15	6
Western Halifax,	25	24	24	380	13	6	423	7	10	804	1	4	201	4	4	203	10	—	404	14	4	1	19	9
Lunenburg,	57	56	48	384	13	8	379	18	2	764	11	10	313	10	—	313	10	—	627	—	—	1	4	4½
Queen's County,	27	33	—	434	11	11	415	13	11	850	5	10	233	—	—	245	—	—	478	—	—	1	17	9
Annapolis,	50	66	—	907	3	8	815	17	2	1723	—	10	361	6	3	349	10	—	710	6	3	2	8	5½
King's County,	50	63	—	814	16	4	927	16	11	1742	13	3	327	10	0	352	—	3	679	10	3	2	11	3
Northern Pictou,*	100	50	60	1476	10	—	790	—	—	2266	10	—	565	-	—	269	—	—	834	—	—	2	14	2½
Southern Pictou,	—	51	51	—	—	—	893	2	6	893	2	6				278	2	1	278	2	1	3	4	3
Parrsborough,	9	9	—	85	12	6	123	—	—	208	12	6	51	2	1½	51	14	—	102	16	1½	2	—	10
Northern Cumberland,	52	54	70	856	14	3	863	—	—	1719	14	3	239	2	5	240	15	3	479	17	8	3	11	7½
Southern Colchester,	49	65	70	675	3	—	970	15	7	1645	18	10	227	10	6	227	11	8	455	1	8	3	12	4
Stirling,	16	15	18	204	13	7	229	1	—	433	14	7	67	4	—	67	4	—	134	8	—	3	4	9
Eastern Hants,	15	22	33	281	10	10	337	3	7	618	14	5	110	4	—	110	4	—	220	8	—	2	16	3
Western Hants,	29	33	—	539	8	10	625	10	8	1164	19	6	211	5	10	218	17	7	430	3	5	2	14	2
Clare,	13	19	—	143	16	10	192	2	4½	335	19	2½	73	15	6	75	7	6½	159	3	0½	2	2	3
Northern Digby,	27	39	27	567	17	4	646	19	6	1217	16	10	—	—	—	—	—	—	408	13	4	2	18	8½
Yarmouth,	28	33	33	519	12	6	449	15	10¼	969	8	4½	169	14	2½	163	—	3	332	14	5½	2	18	4½
Argyle,	9	18	26	82	10	—	161	14	9	244	4	9	46	5	—	93	10	—	139	15	—	1	14	10½
Barrington,	13	18	26	127	10	11½	201	16	8½	329	7	8	92	10	—	105	15	—	198	5	—	1	13	3½
Shelburne,	21	21	—	214	16	—	161	10	9	376	6	9	122	10	—	122	19	—	245	—	—	1	10	8½
St. Mary's,	9	11	17	98	13	2½	90	2	4	188	15	6½	57	—	—	55	—	—	112	—	—	1	13	8½
Eastern Guysboro',	26	31	39	358	9	10	377	15	4	736	5	2	168	11	4	177	14	4	346	5	8	2	2	6
Sydney,	49	54	—	548	3	9½	577	19	10	1126	3	7½	329	15	11½	336	8	4½	667	4	4	1	13	9½
Southern Inverness,	47	41	50	460	12	5	373	6	8	833	19	1	244	18	7	248	13	4½	493	11	11½	1	13	10
Northern Inverness,	26	24	36	238	6	10	222	11	7	460	18	5	121	5	8	122	16	—	244	1	8	1	17	9½
Cape Breton and Victoria, Richmond,	38	32	38	288	14	6	261	12	1	550	6	7	202	4	6	209	2	6½	411	7	0½	1	7	0½
Totals and Averages,	825	1004	712	11459	18	2½	11942	15	10½	23402	14	1	5073	11	7½	5186	11	0½	10668	16	0	2	4	7
† Do. for 1850,	886	843		9645	1	6	11236	17	5½	25139		8½	3863	19	8½	4892	11	2½	10592	2	1	2	4	3

* The first half year includes the whole county

† In winter half year of 1850 there were no returns from some districts.

TABLE II.—*Number, Age and Sex of Pupils—Number of Children in Districts.*

DISTRICTS.	Paid Pupils.		Free Pupils.		Total Pupils.		Ages of Pupils.				Sex of Pupils.				Chil. fm. 4 to 15 in district	School sec. not report'g.
	Winter.	Sum'r.	W.	S.	W.	S.	Under 8. W.	S.	Over 8. W.	S.	Males. W.	S.	Females. W.	S.		
City of Halifax,	808	913	744	719	1552	1720	529	632	1023	1075	852	884	700	835	4500	6
Eastern Halifax,	864	799	56	69	920	868	189	284	630	584	430	433	379	435	1114	1
Western Halifax,	973	1100	74	122	1020	1222	237	361	820	871	635	682	408	542	1934	6
Lunenburgh,	1314	1101	228	164	1542	1265	305	407	1237	850	928	672	614	593	2642	
Queen's County,	749	765	109	153	858	916	108	261	750	635	537	492	321	424	1335	
Annapolis,	1467	1636	263	309	1730	1981	274	379	1424	1416	1130	1054	568	994	3248	
King's County,	1570	1591	320	456	1890	2047	293	666	1597	1381	1260	922	630	1125	3199	
Northern Pictou,	4073	1994	295	163	4368	2157	810	622	3542	1520	2507	1126	1843	1016	2663	
Southern Pictou,		2513		169		2682		721		1961		1494		1188	3232	10
Parrsborough,	177	150	51	20	228	170	56	72	169	121	122	89	83	102	297	1?
Northern Cumberland,	1614	1727	239	218	1853	1945	513	707	1341	1238	1078	1045	775	900	2010	23
Southern Colchester,	1413	1751	116	142	1526	1893	341	649	1053	1196	867	1015	629	882	1295	33
Stirling,	639	578	55	33	694	611	161	86	533	525	387	378	307	233	1032	3
Eastern Hants,	479	678	46	63	572	841	91	200	471	507	319	398	243	346	915	11
Western Hants,	816	948	118	153	934	1101	164	283	922	818	623	525	337	576	1803	
Clare,	281	375	67	104	348	479	43	97	305	382	195	220	153	259	1068	
Northern Digby,	787	909	154	164	941	1073	136	262	885	811	677	526	264	547	1818	4
Yarmouth,	854	866	220	269	1076	1135	151	389	925	746	823	596	253	539	2190	8
Argyle,	177	390	55	100	222	490	35	146	187	344	151	236	71	273	911	8
Barrington,	287	353	60	91	347	444	59	150	288	294	257	212	90	232	705	
Shelburne,	468	364	49	63	514	426	93	155	429	270	329	205	181	221	784	8
St. Mary's,	194	199	39	28	233	227	49	65	178	147	153	137	64	78	336	15
Eastern Guysborough,	533	710	121	194	755	967	148	269	606	696	440	494	322	473	1212	12?
Sydney,	1272	1413	192	191	1464	1604	189	278	1279	1326	898	937	566	667	1565	8
Southern Inverness,	1139	950	193	184	1332	1134	121	179	1211	955	901	738	431	396	2147	10
Northern Inverness,	622	531	98	77	720	608	94	112	626	496	475	383	245	225	1288	
Cape Breton and Victoria,																
Richmond,	699	616	297	295	996	911	186	220	777	639	572	537	424	375	1642	
Totals,	24269	25918	4259	4713	28528	30631	5375	9352	23205	21835	17537	16430	10901	14470	46886	
Do. in 1850,	21219	23391	2599	3917	22818	27838	2596	7476	11183	19308	9101	14989	5538	11634		
	4193	748			4941		874		2329		1749		1377			

TABLE III.—*Average Attendance—Duration of Schools—Sex and Salary of Teachers.*

DISTRICT.	Average attendance, winter.	Average No. on list, winter.	Avg. No. from 4 to 15 in district.	Duration of Schools. W. weeks.	Duration of Schools. S. weeks.	Sex of Teachers. Male. W.	Male. S.	Female. W.	Female. S.	Average salaries of Teachers. From People.	From Province.	Total.
City of Halifax,	76.	110	285.7	21¼	22¼	9	9	5	5	£49 2 6	£48 18 6	£98 1 10
Eastern Halifax,	15 5	28.7	33.1	24	22	22	19	4	8	27 8 0	15 9 1	42 17 1
Western Halifax,	28.4	40.8	87.8	19¾	22½	22	20	3	4	33 10 0	16 17 3	50 7 3
Lunenburg,	16.8	27.	46 3	22½	22½	32	29	25	27	13 13 0½	11 4 0	24 17 0½
Queen's County,		31 8	58.	19½	23½	21	14	6	18	28 0 10	13 0 0	41 0 10
Annapolis,	17.5	34.6	57.4	22½	22¾	42	39	8	27	29 14 1½	12 5 1	41 19 2½
King's County,	20.2	31.4	53.2	21¼	23	42	31	8	32	31 2 4	12 2 8	43 5 0
[illegible]u,	23.4	40.7	43.6	21½	21½	88	89	12	12	31 11 9	11 2 4	42 14 1
Parrsborough,	13.4	25 3	33.	[illegible]½	19½	6	7	3	2	23 3 7	11 8 5	34 12 0
Northern Cumberland,	19 5	32 2	38.1	22	22	45	44	7	10	32 9 0½	9 0 9	41 9 9½
Southern Colchester,	17.7	31.1	40.4	19½	21½	36	35	13	39	29 1 0½	8 0 0	37 1 0½
Stirling,	21.1	43.3	68.8	20½	22	14	14	2	1	28 18 8	8 19 2	37 17 10
Eastern Hants,	23.	38.1	45.7	22¾	20	13	13	2	9	34 7 9	12 4 5	46 12 2
Western Hants,	19.2	32.2	48	22½	23¾	21	18	8	15	37 11 7	13 17 5	50 8 1½
Clare,	18.4	26.7	60.	19	19	8	5	5	14	21 0 0	9 18 9	30 18 9
Digby,	26 8	35.	72.7	21¼	20½	22	21	5	18	36 18 2	12 6 0½	49 4 2½
Yarmouth,	27.	38 4	73.5	19	21½	24	9	4	24	32 6 0	11 2 0	43 8 0
Argyle,	23.4	27 7	40.9	15¼	21½	8	8		10	18 15 4	10 15 4	29 10 8
Barrington,	20.4	26.7	42.3	18	23	9	6	4	12	21 12 0	14 10 8	36 2 8
Shelburne,	18.4	24.4	56.	20	22¾	13	7	9	15	17 13 4	11 13 4	29 6 8
St. Mary's,	14.6	25.8	28.6	19	18½	9	7		4	18 18 7	11 4 0	30 2 7
Eastern Guysboro',	18.3	28.6	50.2	23½	22½	21	23	5	8	26 5 8	12 7 1½	38 12 9½
Sydney,	18.7	29.8	46.	22½	22½	38	40	11	14	22 1 7½	13 1 7½	35 3 3
Southern Inverness,	18.3	30 3	52.2	23	21¼	44	38	3	3	18 18 7	11 4 6½	30 3 1½
Northern Inverness,	19.6	27.6	53.6		20¾	23	20	3	4	18 8 9	9 19 4½	28 8 1½
Cape Breton,												
Richmond,	20.	26.4	63.1			30	23	8	9	15 14 3	11 15 10	27 10 1
Totals and Averages,	21.4	32.7	58.7			662	588	163	344	25 9 10	13 1 9½	38 11 7½
Do. 1850,	23.9	32.5	52.8			718	604	149	321	24 15 3	11 11 10½	36 7 1½

TABLE IV.—*Character of Schools—Apparatus—School Houses.*

District.	Grammar Schools.	Schools teaching classics or math'cs.	Schls. not teaching gram'r. or geography	Schools having reg's. of errors and merits	Schools having Globes.	Schools having wall maps.	Schools having black boards.	Schools having other apparatus.	Total Schools, winter.	SCHOOL HOUSES.							
										Under 18x20 feet.	Under 20x30	20x30 and over.	Frame.	Log.	In good repair.	Unfinish'd or in bad repair.	Having "new furniture."
City of Halifax,	1	8			5	10	9	7	14	15	6	14			14		3
Eastern Halifax,	1		4	5		6	9	3	26	7	11	3	15	5	21	3	
West'n Halifax,	3		4	6		18	8	2	25	24	24	4	24	1	21	3	
Lunenburg,	2	2	32	6	2	11	9	1	57	5	8	3	33		51	2	
Queen's County	4	1	8	4	2	4	4	2	27	10	29	7	21		22		
Annapolis	3	18	3	1	3	6	10		50	18	22	1	45	1	42	7	
King's County,	2	2		18		11	15		50	21	21	3	44	2	40	7	
N. Pictou,	2	6	12	2	1	20	26	1	50	22	23	3	36	10	40	6	2
S. Pictou,		12	16	13	2	23	21	1	51	7	1		43	8	43	5	2
Parrsborough,		1	4	2		7	9		9	7	25	2	7	2	1	8	3
Cumberland,	3	3	16	17	1	28	11	2	52	17	20	2	50	2	52	1	
S. Colchester,		11	9	7		7	9		49	5	8	1	33	1	32	2	
Stirling,		2		6	1	8	4	2	16	7	6		10	6	11	5	
E. Hants,		5	2	4		4	3		15	5	12	4	14		12	2	3
W. Hants,	2	9	7	5	1				29	11	7		25		24	5	
Clare,		2	9	3	2	4	4		13	7	8	2	19	2	14	5	
N. Digby,	2	7	3	5	2	6	14		27	7	19						1
Yarmouth,	1	7	9	10			3		28	6	3	2	28		24	4	1
Argyle,		2	4				6		9	2	5	6	7		8	1	1
Barrington,	1	2	7	4	1	5	2		18	13	1		16	2	14	4	
Shelburne,	1	4	12	5	1	1	5		21	5	3		16		17		1
St. Mary's,		3	1	1	1	3	4	2	11	3	3	1	6	3	5		
E. Guysboro',		1	10		1	18	7		26	14	16		16	10	17	4	
Sydney,	2	9	28	4		6	7		49	26	9	2	32	16	39	9	1
S. Inverness,	2	3	24		1	6	7		47	30	4		6	40	13	7	
N. Inverness,		3	12	15	1	7		1	26	21			9	17	13	34	
Cape Breton,																13	
Richmond,		2	26	12	1	2	2		38	21	2		9	28			
Totals,	**31**	**125**	**262**	**155**	**29**	**221**	**208**	**24**	**825**	**334**	**287**	**58**	**567**	**156**	**590**	**137**	**18**
Do. 1850,	**25**	**102**	**384**	**46**	**16**	**118**	**109**	**13**	**912**	**215**	**216**	**51**	**443**	**115**	**444**	**125**	

TABLE V.—*Abstract of Returns of Grammar Schools.*

Name of District	Teacher and Place	No. of Pupils Winter Pd.	Winter Fr.	Summer Pd.	Summer Fr.	Average attend. W.	S.	Pupils in higher branches W.	S.	Support from District	Support from Province	Globes	W. Maps	B.boards	Dimensions of House	Higher Branches Taught
E. Halifax,	A. Russell, Musquodoboit,	55	12	59	12	35	41	16	17	50 0 0	47 10 0	0	10	2	29x18	Geometry, Agr. Chemistry
W. Halifax,	J. Davison, Sackville,	81	1	39	12	27		12		22 16 0	23 15 0	0		1	30x30	Latin, Geometry Algebra
Lunenburgh,	W. B. Lawson, Lunenburg,	39	12	61	12	40	40			50 0 0	40 0 0	2	12	1	38x32	Latin, Alg., Math., Ag. Chem.
"	J. McKinnon, Chester,	61	2	51	2	48	48			40 0 0	30 0 0	2	12	1	30x20	Algebra, Math., Ag. Chem.
"	H. D. Marshall, Bridgewater,	51	10	40	10	40	40			40 0 0	30 0 0	0	7	1	35x15	Latin, Algebra, Mathematics
Queen's Co.	Jas. Parker, Liverpool,	58	11	35	14			19	19	98 10 0	47 10 0	0	6	2	18x27	Alg., Math., Agr. Chemistry
"	J. E. Balcom, Port Medway,	49	8	54	10	24	39	14	17	47 10 0	47 10 0	0		1		Alg., Math., Agr. Chemistry
Annapolis,	H. Deblois, Annapolis,	25				24				68 0 0	25 0 0	0	6	1	36x21	Latin, Greek, French, Math.
"	W. Shipley, Bridgetown,	49	5	28		42		13		64 0 0	25 0 0	0			60x30	Latin, Mathematics.
"	J. W. Hart, Paradise,	68	2	54		40				37 10 0	12 10 0	0	1	1	35x24	Latin, Greek, Algebra, Math.
"	J. Phinney, Nictaux,	23	7	22		25	35	50	31	75 0 0	25 0 0	0	1	1	24x30	Latin, Alg., Math., Ag. Ch.
N. Pictou,	D. McDonald, West River,	61	3	65	5	27	30	14	15	50 0 0	25 0 0	0	4	2	28x25	Latin, Greek, Math., Ag. Ch.
"	C. E. Henry, River John,	53	5	50		45	30	16	14	70 0 0	25 0 0	0	2	1	17x21	Latin, French
S. Pictou,	J. McKay, New Glasgow,	52	6	64	3	45	50	16	12	105 0 0	36 13 4	0	1	1	24x30	Latin, Alg., Math., Agr. Ch.
"	J. Fraser, Merigonish,	81		65	3	42	38	55	12	40 0 0	19 15 0	0	1	1	22x24	Latin, French, Alg., Agr. Ch.
Cumberland,	S. O'Donnell, Amherst,	61	1	53		42		19	10	50 0 0	23 0 0	2		1	21x17	Algebra, Mathematics
"	S. Hart, Hart,	30	5	23	3	25	20	10	10	48 15 0	21 4 0	0	2	1	24x20	Latin, Algebra, Mathematics
W. Hants,	D. McKay, Wallace,	77	17	84	15	56	45	31	31	50 0 0	26 5 0	0	3	1	22x18	Algebra, Math., Agr. Chem.
"	B. Curran, Windsor,	42	6	36	8	40		16	14	119 3 4	31 13 4	2		1	30x29	Latin, Greek, Alg., French
"	G. F. McDonald, Newport,	41	9	45	8	27	30	11	11	118 6 8	31 13 4	0		1	27x18	Algebra, Mathematics
N. Digby,	W. Loudett, Digby,	36	4	33	3	34	30	12	12	100 0 0	41 13 4	0	6	1	22x32	Latin, Mathematics, French
"	T. Meldon, Weymouth,	50		44		33	26	13	13	130 0 0	25 0 0	0	12		26x20	Mathematics
Yarmouth,	G. Christie, Yarmouth,	39	3	34	1	28	27	26	14	76 18 0	56 0 0	0	2	2	28x28	Latin, Mathematics, French
Barrington,	J. Urquhart, Barrington,	38	6	36	4	35			6	60 4 0	43 15 0	0	4	1	16x22	Algebra, Mathematics
Shelburne,	J. Freeman, Locke's Island,	43	3	46	5			34		40 0 0	50 0 0	0	6		20x20	Algebra, Mathematics
Guysboro',	T. R. Russell, Guysboro',	36	8	32	9		26	15	12	36 13 4	34 8 9	2		3	30x16	Algebra, Math., Agr. Chem.
"	J. Sutherland, Cape Canseau,	49	9	41	11			10	12	47 0 0	28 17 11	0		3	20x32	Latin, French, Mathematics
Sydney,	R. McDonald, Antigonish,	35	1	36	1	22	26	11	8	20 0 0	47 3 0	0	1	1	25x30	Latin, Greek, Mathematics
"	J. McKinnon, St Andrews,	31	2			33		11		13 6 0	25 0 0	0		1	25x25	Latin, Greek, Algebra
"	W. Chisholm,			32			19		9	30 10 0	17 6 2	0	1	2	23x23	Latin, Algebra, Mathematics
King's,	J. E. Barnaby, Cornwallis,	59	5			31		25		30 0 0	13 10 0	0	1	1	23x22	Mathematics, &c.
"	W. Eaton, junr, Kentville,	41	9	35	10	33	29	10	8	53 10 0	45 0 0	2		1	22x22	Latin, Mathematics, &c.
"	A. M. Patterson, Aylesford,	46	5	28		28		13		23 0 0	14 0 0	0	1	1	18x26	Mathematics, &c.
	Rev. W. Somerville, Cornwallis,			38	10		28		37	30 0 0	20 0 0	0				Heb., Gk, Lat., Math., Alg., &c.
	H. Kerr, Aylesford.			57	7		35		4	22 10 0	25 0 0	0	1	1	24x20	Mathematics, Algebra

APPENDIX.

(A) MINUTES OF EDUCATIONAL MEETINGS.

ANNAPOLIS.

REPORT of a Meeting held at Bridgetown, in the county of Annapolis, by J. W. Dawson, esquire, Superintendent of Education, on the 25th April, 1851.

Most of the Commissioners were present, as well as a considerable number of Teachers, and other persons.

The Superintendent of education addressed the meeting, in a speech, exceedingly clear and comprehensive, on the subject of education generally, and more particularly upon the necessity of having one central Normal or Training School established in the province, and also of carrying out the assessment principle fully. The meeting was then ably addressed by the Rev. Mr. Robertson and Major Chipman, esquire; and a resolution, moved by the Rev. Mr. Robertson, to the following effect, seconded by Thomas James, esquire :—

Resolved, That it is desirable that a Normal School should be established in some convenient part of the province, for the purpose of giving uniformity to our provincial system of education.

This resolution was also supported by Joseph Wheelock, esquire, and by Mr. George Munroe, in speeches appropriate to the occasion. The resolution passed unanimously.

Mr. John Currel then addressed the meeting, and moved the following resolution, which was seconded by Mr. McCan.

Resolved, That it is desirable a system of assessment shall be hereafter adopted by the Legislature, either generally, or in some modified form as shall be found most desirable—which also passed unanimously.

W. H. TROOP, Clerk.

Bridgetown, August 25, 1851.

NORTHERN DISTRICT OF DIGBY.

The Superintendent of Schools held an Educational Meeting at Digby, on Thursday, the 1st day of May, 1851. The meeting was attended by some of the school commissioners, teachers, and other inhabitants of the town and county. The Superintendent addressed the meeting, and with his usual energy endeavoured to impress the paramount subject of general education on the minds of his audience. He dwelt at length on the subject of general taxation as the only sure and efficient scheme for the permanent diffusion of education throughout the province.

At the conclusion of his address the following resolution was proposed by James H. FitzRandolph, esquire, seconded by Laughlan McKay, esquire, and passed unanimously :—

Resolved, That it is the opinion of this meeting, that it is highly desirable that legislative aid should be provided for the establishment of a Normal Training School, and that the system of taxation should be adopted for the support of education throughout the province.

The Rev. Mr. Cunningham, in a short but appropriate speech, addressed the audience in approbation of what had been advanced by the Superintendent. The meeting was then adjourned until seven o'clock in the evening, when Mr. Dawson again delivered an eloquent and appropriate lecture on the same subject.

WM. LOUDETT,
Clerk to Commissioners of Schools,
County of Digby.

DISTRICT OF CLARE.

Pursuant to notice given by J. W. Dawson, esquire, superintendent of education, a meeting was held at the session house in Clare, at 12 o'clock, the 7th day of May, 1851.

A considerable number of persons attended the meeting, including the commissioners, and many teachers and trustees. An eloquent address was given by the Superintendent on the nature of education, the importance of good instruction, and the evil of ignorance. Mr. Dawson also addressed the meeting at some length in favor of a Normal School, established in the province, for the education of teachers.

He also alluded to the principle of assessment, and spoke of the benefits which would arise in getting up and sustaining schools by taxation on the inhabitants of the school districts.

The Revd. Mr. Geary addressed the meeting at great length, explaining in French, with much force, his views in approbation of the lecturer. Mr. Bourneuf made also a few remarks on the subject.

No resolutions followed.

After a few further remarks from Mr. Dawson, the meeting adjourned.

LOUIS Q. BOURQUE, Clerk.

DISTRICT OF ARGYLE.

ARGYLE, 16th MAY, 1851.

Agreeably to notice previously given, the Superintendent of Schools for the Province of Nova Scotia, held a meeting this day in the Court House in Tusket Village, at 11 o'clock, a. m., at which there were only three of the commissioners present, several teachers, and a considerable number of the inhabitants.

Mr. Dawson addressed the meeting at some length on the subject of education generally, in which he strongly recommended the utility of having competent teachers employed in our schools; also the necessity there was for having training schools established in the province for the purpose of qualifying teachers.

John Ryder, Esquire, and several other gentlemen spoke in favour of the subjects advanced by the superintendent of education.

MATTHEW JEFFERY, Clerk.

DISTRICT OF YARMOUTH.

YARMOUTH, MAY 12, 1851.

The annual educational meeting appointed by law, was held by Mr. Dawson, in the Court House, after having been fully advertised in the newspapers and by hand-bills.

An admirable address from Mr. Dawson was delivered to an assemblage of upwards of 120 persons.

An animated discussion followed, principally on the subject of a Normal School and assessment.

Two resolutions were offered,—the first by Dr Farish, "that the establishment of a Normal School in this Province is necessary for the benefit of general education," passed unanimously,—the second by John Murray, esquire, "that the opinion of this meeting is favourable to the principle of general assessment," also passed by a majority, there appearing, on a show of hands, 34 in favour of the resolution, and 17 against it.

G. J. FARISH, Clerk.

DISTRICT OF BARRINGTON.

In conformity with the 23rd section of the act for the encouragement of education, an Educational Meeting was held at the Town
House, Barrington, on Monday, May 19, 1851, at 11 o'clock, a. m.

J. W. Dawson, esquire, superintendent of education presided.
A considerable number of persons attended, including commissioners and teachers.

Mr. Dawson opened the business of the meeting by stating that
the object of calling such meetings as the present, was to advance
the interest of education—to stir up the public mind, and to elicit
and circulate information, and invited persons present to lay their
views before the meeting.

An animated discussion followed on the subject of assessment,
and the benefit arising from the appointment of a general superintendent of education.

Dr. T. O. Geddes moved the following resolution:

Resolved, That the principle of assessment is the only practicable
method of supporting an efficient system of education for the whole
people, which passed by a show of hands, eight being the majority
in favor of assessment.

Resolution moved by W. Sargent, esquire, and passed unanimously.

Resolved, That this meeting feel it a duty to express their high
approval of the appointment of a general superintendent of education for the Province, and contemplate from the brief experience
of the past, much advantage for the future.

Mr. Dawson also lectured in the evening to a large and attentive
assembly, on the benefit arising from an improved system of education. At the close of which lecture the following resolution was
moved by the Rev. W. Wilson, and passed unanimously:—

Resolved, That this meeting aware of the importance of having
properly qualified teachers, approve of the establishment of a Normal School, in which the requisite qualifications may be imparted.

JAMES M. DOANE, Clerk.

Barrington, May 9, 1851.

QUEEN'S COUNTY.

Pursuant to notice previously given, the Superintendent of education called his second meeting in this county, on the 2nd day of
June, at the Temperance Hall in Liverpool.

The meeting, owing to the day being a holyday, was small.
The Superintendent however, delivered an excellent address, calling the attention of the meeting, as on a former occasion, to the
present defective state of education in the Province; and using

many powerful arguments to arouse the people to a higher sense of the necessity of its improvement. S. P. Fairbanks, esquire, also addressed the meeting, and showed that though the present system is defective, much good had resulted from it. At the solicitation of John Campbell, esquire, M. P. P., and others, Mr. Dawson delivered a highly interesting and excellent address upon the various subjects connected with his office, in the presence of a large audience in the evening. ·

CHARLES MORSE, Clerk.

Liverpool, Sept. 1851.

COUNTY OF LUNENBURG.

Pursuant to notice given, and in conformity with the 23d section of the act passed for the "encouragement of education," a public educational meeting was held by John W. Dawson, esquire, Superintendent, in the Court House in Lunenburg, on Friday 7th June, A. D., 1851.

Commissioners present—Revd. William Duff, Chairman; Revd. James C. Cochran, John Heckman, George Ernst, William Ross, and Lemuel Drew, esquires.

Many of the inhabitants of the county, together with several teachers, were also present.

The Superintendent addressed the meeting, as he stated, under the direction of the school act now in operation, and in the hope of hearing some suggestions having a tendency to improve the new law to be passed at the next meeting of the General Assembly. He earnestly invited discussion on the subject of education, and expressed the desire that the friends of education then present, would freely make known their sentiments.

The Revd. Mr. Duff, Chairman of Board of School Commissioners, then addressed the meeting at considerable length, expressing himself much gratified with the eloquent and useful address of the Superintendent, and gave it as his decided opinion that much benefit would result to the cause of education, by the course adapted by Mr. Dawson. He, Mr. Duff, highly approved of the establishment of a Normal School, and expressed the hope that such an institution would soon be found in this Province for the training of duly qualified teachers : he wished it to be perfectly understood that he was in favor of the system of assessment for the support of schools, and requested permission to move the following resolution :

Resolved, That the general assessment principle be approved of as the soundest basis for the support of education in this Province : which resolution, on being seconded and put by the Superintendent, passed.

Lemuel Drew, esquire, commissioner of schools, then addressed the meeting, at some length, and among other things stated, that a meeting of the inhabitants lately held at Petite Riviere, in this county, a resolution, after considerable discussion, had passed, approving of the principle of general assessment for the support of schools.

John Keddy, esquire, M. P., also addressed the meeting, approving of the system of assessment for the support of education.

John Heckman, esquire, commissioner of schools, expressed himself much pleased with the opening address of Mr. Dawson, and felt satisfied in his own mind that much benefit would result from it to the rising generation; and expressed his fears that the assessment system would not work well in this county.

Mr. Matthew Ernst, in a short address, stated that he disapproved of the proposed system of assessment, and gave it as his decided opinion that the House of Assembly would act wisely by giving double the present allowance to each county, for the support of schools.

Rev. Mr. Duff then moved the following resolution: which, on being seconded by Henry S. Jost, esquire, with some appropriate remarks, was put by the chairman, and passed unanimously:

Resolved, That in the opinion of this meeting, the establishment of a Provincial Normal School would be very beneficial in improving the qualifications of teachers, and increasing their remuneration, and the efficiency of their work.

The Revd. James C. Cochran, then addressed the meeting at considerable length, and expressed himself decidedly in favor of the resolution introduced by the Revd. Mr. Duff, and expressed the hope that the day was not far distant when the purport of both resolutions would be carried into effect in this Province. He highly eulogised the address of Mr. Dawson, and stated that, in his opinion, the appointment of the superintendent of education for this Province was a wise measure, and that the choice made had been a happy one, and felt satisfied that the rising generation would be much benefitted by the exertions and zeal of the present superintendent.

After some very interesting and appropriate remarks from Mr. Dawson, he gave notice of holding teachers' meetings at the National School House on the following day, when he fully expected a good and punctual attendance of the teachers of this county. The meeting then adjourned.

DANIEL OWEN, Clerk.

WESTERN DISTRICT OF HALIFAX.

Agreeably to public notice, an educational meeting for the Western District of .Halifax was held this day, at 11 o'clock, A. M., in the Hall of the Mechanics' Institute, at Dartmouth. J. W. Dawson, esquire, provincial superintendent of education, presided. The Rev. Alexander Hichborne and the Rev. P. G. McGregor, two of the school commissioners for the district, were present. Mr. Dawson opened the meeting by stating that it was called for the purpose of eliciting the opinions of persons present, and discussing the great subject of 'education ; and that although the attendance was small, yet the influence of a few, if well directed, might produce important results. Mr. D. explained the objects of the Bill for the founding of a Normal School, which had been thrown out in the last session of the Legislature, and shewed the necessity existing for the establishment of such an institution for the purpose of training teachers and keeping pace with all the improvements that have been made in the art of teaching. The state of the schools in the district was examined, by which it appeared that there was much room for improvement. Mr. Dawson remarked that the commissioners had done much to raise the standard of teaching, and that the salaries of the teachers and the apparatus of the schools compared favorably with other districts. The assessment principle, as applied to education, was treated of at length, and the necessity of its adoption strenuously enforced. He was glad to see a number of teachers in attendance, and addressed them as to the importance of their profession, calling upon them to associate themselves together for the purpose of mutual improvement.

Mr. S. Selden, principal of Acadian School, Halifax, entered into explanations touching the teachers' association which had been organized in the city, and invited the teachers present to attach themselves to the society.

Edward H. Lowe, esq., addressed the meeting, stating that he was not prepared for the *expose* which had been made by Mr. Dawson of the state of education in the district, and thought that one fact had been overlooked—that many of the children were attending private schools. He was afraid the people would not submit to assessment, unless the strong arm of the Legislature interfered and obliged them to pay. He thought assessment for education should be incorporated with that for poor and county rates, and the money made payable in the same way to the county treasurer.

Rev. A. Hichborne then addressed the meeting, stating that he thought with Mr. Lowe that the majority of the people in the province were opposed to assessment for education. He felt the truth of the principle that " property should pay for education," and

shewed that there was only one State in the American Union
which possessed a larger amount of property in proportion to the
number of inhabitants than Nova Scotia.   He regretted that in
some of the school districts there was a great lack of public spirit
respecting education, and thought the law should step in and
oblige the inhabitants to pay for the instruction of their children.
He held that men had no natural or moral right to allow the youth
under their charge to grow up in ignorance, and he trusted that
the remarks of Mr. Dawson on this important subject would carry
with them the influence which belonged to them.   He thought the
members of the Legislature on this as on many questions deeply
affecting the welfare of the people paid too much attention to the
wishes of their constituents—that one great reason why Nova
Scotia was so far in the rear of the position she ought to occupy
was that the blessings of education were not rightly appreciated by
her people—that there should be a general law enforcing a liberal
assessment throughout the province, and that all the schools
should be free, and that every dollar expended in supporting education might be expected to return twofold.   The rev. gentleman
concluded by saying that he would be happy to lend his influence
to bring about a better state of things than had heretofore existed.

The Rev. P. G. McGregor was glad to see so many teachers in
attendance, as it proved that they were desirous of improvement.
That the Board of Commissioners had several times examined the
teachers in their district, and that in all cases where they saw a
desire for improvement they had encouraged it. and had only re-
jected those who were altogether unfit for the profession they had
embraced.   He thought much might be done towards improvement,
by the commissioners inspecting the schools and stimulating and
encouraging the teachers.

The meeting having been addressed by Messrs. Alex. McDonald
and Donald McLean, two of the teachers present, was then adjourned.

MATHER B. DESBRISAY,
Clerk to Commissioners.

EASTERN DISTRICT OF HALIFAX.

The Superintendent of Education held an educational meeting
this day, in the north school-house, Middle Musquodoboit.   Judg-
ing from the interest felt in the cause of education, by the inhabitants of this district generally, the meeting was not so well attended as might have been expected.   Mr. Dawson opened the meeting by referring to the one held last year, and to the resolutions
then passed.   He regretted that the bill for establishing a Normal
School had been lost in the House; and after explaining the ad-

vantages arising from general assessment and a Normal School, he asked the meeting if they still held the same opinions as expressed in their resolutions last year,—invited all to express their opinions and either confirm or reject them. After some remarks from several gentlemen expressive of their adhesion to those resolutions, the following were passed unanimously:

Moved by Mr. Thos. Jamison, and seconded by Adams Archibald, esquire:

Resolved, That this meeting having heard from the Superintendent the nature of the bill submitted, for the Normal School, to the Legislature at its last session, cannot but express their deep regret that it failed to pass into a law, and hope that it may succeed at the next meeting.

Moved by Mr. Alexr. Russell, and seconded by Mr. J. Farquhar:

Resolved, That this meeting would recommend to all the teachers throughout this district the propriety of availing themselves of the advantages resulting from attendance on teachers' institutes.

T. ROBINSON,
Clerk of Commrs.

Musquodoboit, 28th June, 1851.

EASTERN DISTRICT OF HANTS.

Pursuant to notice given, an educational meeting was held on the 24th day of June, 1851, in the Presbyterian church, Kennetcook, the Superintendent presiding.

Messrs. Withrow, Scott, and O'Brien, Commissioners, were present, besides other inhabitants and teachers.

The Superintendent addressed the meeting, referring to various measures of educational improvement, and to the present state of the schools in the district.

The address was heard with the highest satisfaction, when it was moved by W. O'Brien, esq., seconded by J. Withrow, esq., and resolved unanimously,—

" That the establishment of a Normal School would be of essential service to the education of this Province."

Moved by Mr. ———, seconded by J. Withrow, esquire, and passed by a large majority,—

" That in the opinion of this meeting the principle of assessment is sound, and should be established by law as soon as possible."

After some concluding remarks from the Superintendent the meeting was closed.

COUNTY OF SYDNEY.

ANTIGONISHE, 7th AUGUST, 1852.

Agreeably to notice, Mr. Dawson, superintendent of schools, held his second annual educational meeting at the Court House here, at 11 o'clock, a. m.   Several of the school commissioners and a number of schoolmasters were present.

Mr. Dawson, after having graphically described the state of education throughout Nova Scotia, animadverted on the want of zeal and energy in the cause thereof, but too apparent here, and in several other sections of the Province,—explained the nature and operation of Normal Schools—which he warmly advocated the establishment of, as well as the principle of assessment for schools, of which he largely entered into detail, and also strenuously recommended the formation of a teachers' association in this place.

Some very pertinent remarks were subsequently made by several gentlemen present, and the following resolution, which was passed *nem. con.*, was then moved by the hon. Alexander M'Dougall, and seconded by the Revd. Mr. Trotter:—

Resolved, That in order to secure a constant supply of competent teachers, and to enable the teachers already employed to extend and improve their professional knowledge, a Provincial Normal or Training School for teachers should be established in some central and convenient part of the Province.

In the evening, Mr. D. delivered a lucid and impressive lecture on intellectual training, which was listened to with profound attention, and highly applauded by a respectable audience.

JAMES WILKIE,
Clerk to School Commissioners,
County Sydney.

EASTERN DISTRICT OF GUYSBORO'.

According to previous notice given, an educational meeting was held in the Court House in Guysboro', on Tuesday, the 12th day of August, 1851, at 11 o'clock, A. M.

J. W. Dawson, esq., addressed the meeting, and shewed from the statistics of schools received since last year the deficiency existing throughout the province on the subject of education, and the necessity of devising means for the general benefit of schools: also shewing the great destitution of proper schools in the country—the number of districts without any teachers, in consequence of which a large number of youth were growing up in ignorance—the small sums raised for teachers' salaries, and the great necessity of establishing a seminary in this province for training teachers, &c.

The following resolution was then moved by E. H. Franchville, esquire, and seconded by Mr. John Jost :

Resolved, That it is the opinion of this meeting that in order to extend and diffuse the benefits of a good common school education, and bring the same within the reach of all classes, the system of general assessment (based on equitable principles) should be introduced throughout the province, that being the only practicable way by which so desirable an object can be effected. Previous to the putting of this resolution, John Campbell, esq., moved the following, which was seconded by Stewart Campbell, esq., and passed unanimously :

Resolved, That the establishment of a Normal School be strongly recommended to the consideration of the Provincial Legislature.

Dr. Carritt made some remarks upon both resolutions, and heartily concurred that each should be sustained by the province at large.

Stewart Campbell, esq., then addressed the meeting, and spoke against compulsory assessment,—was willing where a district could agree to assess themselves that they should do so as the present law allows.

After a lengthy discussion from a number of gentlemen present, nearly all of whom supported the first resolution, it was put and passed nearly unanimously, only four voting against it. The meeting was then adjourned, previous to which notice was given by Mr. Dawson that he would lecture on the subject of education, in the evening, at half past seven o'clock.

H. R. CUNNINGHAM,
Clerk to Commissioners.

DISTRICT OF ST. MARY'S.

GLENELG, ST. MARY'S, JULY 31, 1852.

This day an educational meeting was held here. Mr. Dawson, superintendent of education, by whose direction the meeting was convened, presided, and delivered a long and interesting address, in which he adverted to the efforts made during the past year, to improve the schools of this Province,—the necessity for the establishment of a good Normal School for the training of teachers, and the adoption of the assessment principle for the raising of a part of the funds required for the proper support of schools.

After the commissioners and others, had addressed the meeting, and expressed their hearty concurrence in every thing advanced by the Superintendent, the following resolutions passed unanimously :

Moved by H. McDonald, esquire, seconded by Mr. A. Kirk,—

1. That while this meeting views with much satisfaction the efforts made to advance the educational interests of our country last year, it cannot but regret that the Legislature at its last Session did not establish a Normal School in accordance with the plan proposed and recommended by the Superintendent,

Moved by William Bent, esquire, and seconded by John Hattie, esquire.

2. That it is the opinion of this meeting that the cause of common school education will not be raised from its present languishing condition, until our Legislature make it imperative upon the inhabitants to support their schools, in part at least, by assessment.

JOHN CAMPBELL,
Clerk to Commissioners.

COUNTY OF RICHMOND.

In conformity with the 23d section of the Act for the encouragement of Schools, a public educational meeting was held at Arichat on the 19th day of August, pursuant to notice. Present: John W. Dawson, esquire, Superintendent, Rev. James A. Shaw, Rev. E. Chartier, and William Crichton and Andrew Madden, esquires, Commissioners, Rev. Murdoch Stewart, of St. George's Channel, and several gentlemen of the country, interested in the cause of education, including a good number of teachers.

The Superintendent addressed the meeting in his usual happy style on the advantages attending free discussion of all matters connected with education—the disadvantages of the present mode of teaching—recommended the establishment of a Normal or Training School for teachers, and advocated general assessment for the support of teachers.

Rev. Murdoch Stewart addressed the meeting in a lengthy speech,—dwelt upon the responsibility of parents and others entrusted with the training of the youthful mind—advocated the establishment of a Normal or Training School, and recommended general assessment. The rev. gentlemen was listened to with deep attention.

Rev. E. Chartier next addressed the meeting on the general principles of education as now pursued in Canada,—spoke in favor of a Normal or Training School, and cordially agreed with the remarks made by the Superintendent, and was convinced that the system of assessment was the best mode for encouraging education.

After a few observations by several other gentlemen, the following resolutions were submitted, moved, seconded and unanimously passed :

Moved by Rev. Murdoch Stewart and seconded by Mr. John Tyrrel :

Resolved, That it is the opinion of this meeting that until a proper system by means of assessment on equitable principles for the support of education is established, education cannot flourish, and that every proper means be used to impress upon the public mind the advantages of that mode of supporting schools.

Moved by William Crichton, esq., and seconded by James A. Shaw :

Resolved, That it is the opinion of this meeting that the establishment of a Normal School would be highly beneficial to the cause of education by raising the qualification of teachers and increasing the rate of their remuneration ; and that it approves generally of the plan of such Normal School as submitted by the Superintendent.

Moved by John Fuller, esq., and seconded by Mr. John F. Fuller :

Resolved, That the schools in this county demand a better and more cordial support on the part of the people in general, and that their condition might be much improved by the erection of better buildings and greater care on the part of trustees and people in selecting teachers.

The Superintendent then entered largely into the duties and responsibilities of teachers and other matters on education. His remarks were listened to with great attention and satisfaction.

THOMAS H. FULLER, Clerk.

Arichat, August 19, 1851.

* * *

SOUTHERN DISTRICT OF INVERNESS.

In accordance with the 23d section of the act for the encouragement of education, a public educational meeting was held in the academy at Port Hood, on the 8th September, 1851, at which J. W. Dawson, esquire, superintendent of education, presided.

Commissioners present—John L. Tremain, chairman, and Peter Smyth, esquires.

The superintendent addressed the meeting at great length, explaining with much force his views with respect to the important object for which the meeting was called.

Mr. Tremain spoke of the aversion on the part of the people of this county to be assessed for the support of schools, but said he advocated the principle, and urged strongly upon all present to try and make the right impression upon the minds of the people of this county.

Mr. Smyth thought that if the assessment principle should be established, that the tax in country places should be made payable in produce.

There being few others than teachers present, no resolutions were passed. After a few remarks from Mr. Dawson, the meeting adjourned.

JAMES MACDONELL, Clerk.

Port Hood, Sept. 10, 1851.

DISTRICT OF STIRLING.

Pursuant to notice previously given, an educational meeting was held in the School House at Tatamagouche, at which the superintendent presided.

Although the meeting was small, Mr. Dawson delivered a very forcible address on the subject of education, in which he spoke of the state of education in this district, comparing the results as given in the statistical report of last year, with those of the Province generally.

After some remarks by those present on the expediency of assessment for the support of education, and the necessity of a training school, the following resolutions were moved, seconded, and unanimously adopted :—

Resolved, That the commissioners of schools for the district of Stirling, be respectfully requested, at their meeting in November next, to call meetings of the inhabitants in the several school districts under their superintendance, or otherwise to adopt such measures as they think most suitable for ascertaining the minds of the people respecting the support of schools by means of assessment.

Resolved, That in the opinion of this meeting, the interests of education in this Province have been greatly retarded by the rejection of the Normal School Bill during the late Session of the Legislature—that the standard of qualification requisite for teachers of youth ought to be much more elevated than it is at present—that for this purpose a seminary for the training of teachers is essentially necessary, and ought not to be overlooked in the legislative enactments on education at the next session of the Provincial Legislature.

JOHN CURRIE, Clerk of Comm'rs.

AMHERST.

At an educational meeting held at the court house in Amherst, on Tuesday, the 21st October,

Mr. Dawson, the superintendent of education, took the chair, and addressed the meeting upon the rise and progress of education, and recommended a Normal School for the training of teachers and the support of schools by assessment.

Revd. George Townshend spoke in favor of assessment.

John Bent, esquire, addressed the meeting in a favor of a training school and assessment.

Revd. Mr. Francis addressed the meeting.

The following resolution was moved by the Revd. W. C. Beals, and seconded by Thomas Logan, esquire :—

Resolved as the opinion of this meeting, that in order to have an efficient system of education upon a sound and permanent footing, assessment and one Normal School for the tuition of teachers are essential elements.

Elisha B. Cutler, esquire, William P. Moffitt, esquire, and Mr. George Crookshanks, spoke in support of the resolution, when the same was put and carried unanimously.

JOSHUA CHANDLER, Clerk.

January 28, 1852.

PARRSBOROUGH.

An educational meeting was held at the Presbyterian Meeting House at Parrsborough, on the 25th of October, 1851, at which the commissioners of schools, the different school teachers of the district, and a considerably large number of other persons of respectability were present.

Mr. Dawson, the superintendent of schools first addressed the meeting, and ably set forth the propriety of supporting common schools by the system of assessment, to the extent of provincial aid, and the advantages of establishing a Normal School in a central part of the Province.

After the superintendent had closed his address, James Fitzpatrick, esquire, next addressed the meeting, objecting to the assessment on property only, and thought it should be extended to the income of people generally. Ebenezer Kerr and Francis Carroll, esquires, likewise addressed the meeting at some length, and supported the superintendent's views relating to assessment system, and in addition thought it should extend to the whole support requisite with the provincial aid. Mr. Elisha D. W. Ratchford followed, and illustrated by example, as well as argument, the necessity of diffusing education amongst the people generally, and also advocated the system of assessment to the full extent required; and T. D. Dickson, esquire, also delivered his views on the subject, and advocated the mode of assessment on the people to the extent of aid granted by the province, and the propriety of establishing a Normal School.

The two following resolutions were then moved and unanimously adopted.

First—moved by Ebenezer Kerr, esquire, and seconded by Francis Carroll, esquire.

Resolved, That this meeting approve of the system of assessment for the support of common schools, and therefore recommend the Legislature to enact a law which will carry that into effect.

Second—moved by T. D. Dickson, and seconded by E. D. W. Ratchford.

Resolved, That it be recommended to the Legislature to establish a Normal or Training School in some central part of the province, for the preparation of competent teachers.

R. B. DICKSON,
Clerk to the Board of School Commissioners
for the District of Parsborough.

COLCHESTER.

The Superintendent held a public educational meeting at the Court House in Truro, on Monday, the 3d day of November, 1851, at 11 o'clock, A. M., in conformity with the 23d section of the School Act.

Mr. Dawson opened the business of the meeting by an address, embodying a variety of statistical information in reference to the state of education in the province, deducing therefrom much sound argument for the establishment of a provincial Normal School, and support of education by assessment. The meeting was not so well attended as its importance required, attributable to the unfavorable state of the weather.

The Superintendent having closed his address, announced that School Libraries and an additional supply of School Books had recently been furnished to the Board of Education at this place, which would be distributed by the Board at their next meeting, to occur during the present month. Also referred to arrangements for holding a Teachers' Institute in this place, at the academy, during the present week—recapitulating the order of exercises; and also that public lectures would be delivered in this building during the term. The Superintendent then proceeded to take down the names of those who proposed to avail themselves of the instructions at the institute, the number of whom subsequently amounted to 68. The meeting then closed.

GEORGE DILL,
Clerk to Comm'rs. of Schools.

Truro, Nov. 3, 1851.

NEW GLASGOW.

An educational meeting was held at New Glasgow, the 27th January, at which J. W. Dawson, esquire, the superintendent of education, in an able address advocated the principle of assessment for the support of common schools, and the following resolutions were put and unanimously passed :

Moved by Alexr. Fraser, esquire, Middle River, and seconded by James Carmichael, esquire,—

1. *Resolved*, That this meeting recognizes the principle of assessment for the support of common schools, as best adapted to the requirements of this country ; and to enable the Superintendent of Education to obtain the passage of an act embodying that principle agree to append their names to a memorial for that purpose, to be presented to the Provincial Legislature at its approaching session.

Moved by James Carmichael, esquire, and seconded by John McKay, esquire,—

2. *Resolved*, That such petition embody a request that Provincial funds be appropriated for the establishment and support of a Normal School for the training of teachers.

3. *Resolved*, That John McKay, esquire, Mr. John McKay, (teacher,) and Edmund Roach, esquire, be a Committee to prepare such Petition, and have copies forwarded to different localities for signature. .

EDMUND ROACH, Clerk.

NORTHERN DISTRICT OF PICTOU.

PICTOU, JAN. 23, 1852.

An educational meeting was held here this day, in pursuance of notices issued by the superintendent of education.

A very limited number of persons were in attendance,—among these were the Revd. Messrs. Bayne and Herdman, and R. P. Grant, esquire, commissioners of schools.

The superintendent addressed the meeting, giving some statistical information on the state of education for the past year. He brought under the notice of the meeting some details of a bill intended to be submitted to the Legislature, involving the principle of assessment for schools, with other material changes ; also, providing for the establishment of a Provincial Normal School.

In consequence of the small attendance, no resolutions of any kind were offered.

It was then announced by the superintendent that a public meeting would be held at the Assembly Hall, on Tuesday evening, the 3d of February next, for the purpose of laying the subject of education more fully before the public.

M. T. SMITH, Clerk.

(B) EXTRACTS FROM AN ADDRESS ON "THE SYSTEM OF FREE
SCHOOLS," BY REV. E. RYERSON, D. D., CHIEF SUPERINTEN-
DENT OF EDUCATION, UPPER CANADA.

1. My first reason for commending assessment as the best method of providing for the education of your children is, that the
people who have been educated under it for two hundred years, are
distinguished for personal independence, general intelligence, great
industry, economy and prosperity, and a wide diffusion of the comforts and enjoyments of domestic life. The truth of this remark
in reference to the character and condition of the people of the
New England States, will, I presume, be disputed by none. If
their system of civil government be thought less favourable to the
cultivation and exercise of some of the higher virtues than that
which we enjoy, the efficacy of their school system is the more apparent under circumstances of comparative disadvantage. I will
give the origin of this school system in the words of the English
"Quarterly Journal of Education," published under the superin-
tendence of the Society for the Diffusion of Useful Knowledge, and
at a time when Lord Brougham was Chairman and Lord John
Russell Vice-Chairman, of the Committee:

"The first hint of this system—the great principle of which is,
that the property of all shall be taxed by the majority for the education of all—is to be found in the records of the city of Boston for
the year 1635, when at a public or 'body' meeting, a schoolmaster
was appointed 'for the teaching and nurturing of children among
us,' and a portion of the public lands given him for his support.
This, it should be remembered, was done within five years after
the first peopling of that little peninsula, and before the humblest
wants of its inhabitants were supplied, while their very subsistence,
from year to year, was uncertain, and when no man in the colony
slept in his bed without apprehension from the savages, who not
only everywhere crossed their borders, but still dwelt in the
midst of them.

"This was soon imitated in other villages and hamlets springing
up in the wilderness. Winthrop, the earliest governor of the colony and the great patron of Free Schools, says in his journal, under date of 1645, that divers Free Schools were erected in that
year in other towns, and that in Boston it was determined to allow,
for ever, £50 a year to the master, with a house, and £30 to an
usher. But thus far only the individual towns had acted. In

1647, however, the Colonial Assembly of Massachusetts made provision, by law, that every town in which there were fifty families should keep a free school, in which reading and writing could be taught; and every town where there were one hundred families should keep a school where youth could be prepared in Latin, Greek, and Mathematics, for the College or University, which in 1638 had been established by the same authority at Cambridge. In 1656 and 1672 the colonies of Connecticut and New Haven enacted similar laws, and from this time the system spread with the extending population of that part of America until it became one of its settled and prominent characteristics, and has so continued to the present day."

The following extracts from the Annual School Reports of 1847 and 1848, prepared by the Secretary of the Massachusetts Board of Education, deserve special attention, as well for the beauty of their language as for the nobleness of the sentiments which they express :

" The present year (1847) completes the second century since the Free Schools of Massachusetts were first established. In 1647, when a few scattered and feeble settlements, almost buried in the depths of the forests, were all that constituted the colony of Massachusetts ; when the entire population consisted of twenty-one thousand souls ; when the external means of the people were small, their dwellings humble, and their raiment and subsistence scanty and homely; when the whole valuation of all the colonial estates, both public and private, would hardly equal the inventory of many a private individual at the present day ; when the fierce eye of the savage was nightly seen glaring from the edge of the surrounding wilderness, and no defence or succour was at hand; it was then, amid all these privations and dangers, that the Pilgrim Fathers conceived the magnificent idea of a free and universal education for the people ; and, amid all their poverty, they stinted themselves to a still scantier pittance; amid all their toils, they imposed upon themselves still more burdensome labours; amid all their perils, they braved still greater dangers, that they might find the time and the means to reduce their grand conception to practice. Two divine ideas filled their great hearts,—their duty to God and to posterity. For the one, they built the Church; for the other, they opened the School. Religion and Knowledge !—two attributes of the same glorious and eternal truth,—and that truth, the only one on which immortal or mortal happiness can be securely founded.

" As an innovation upon all pre-existing policy and usages, the establishment of Free Schools was the boldest ever promulgated since the commencement of the Christian era. As a theory, it could have been refuted and silenced by a more formidable array of argument and experience than was ever marshalled against any other opinion of human origin. But time has ratified its soundness. Two centuries now proclaim it to be as wise as it was courageous, as beneficent as it was disinterested. It was one of those grand mental and moral experiments whose effects cannot be determined in a single generation. But now, according to the manner in which human life is completed, we are the sixth generation from its founders, and have we not reason to be grateful both to God and man for its unnumbered blessings? The sincerity of our gratitude must be tested by our efforts to perpetuate and improve what they established."—(Tenth Annual Report to the Board of Education, for 1847, pp. 107, 108.)

2. The second ground on which I commend this system of supporting Common Schools to your favorable consideration, is its cheapness to parents educating their children. I will select the example of one district, rather better than an average specimen; and the same mode of reasoning will apply to every district in Upper Canada, and with the same results. In one district there were reported 200 schools in operation in 1848; the average time of keeping open the schools was eight months; the average salaries of teachers was £45 7s. 1d.; the total amount of the money available for the teachers' salaries, including the legislative grant, council assessment and rate-bills, was £7,401 18s. 4½d.; the whole number of pupils between the ages of five and sixteen years on the School registers, was 9,147; the total number of children between those ages resident in the district, 20,600: cost per pupil for eight months, about sixteen shillings. Here it will be seen that more than one-half of the children of school age in the district were not attending any school. Now, suppose the schools be kept open the whole year, instead of two-thirds of it; suppose the male and female teachers to be equal in number, and the salaries of the former to average £60, and those of the latter £40; suppose the 20,600 children to be in the schools instead of 9,147 of them. The whole sum required for the salaries of teachers would be £10,000—the cost per pupil would be less than ten shillings— less than five shillings per inhabitant—which would be reduced still further by deducting the amount of the legislative school grant. Thus would a provision be made for the education of every child in the district for the whole year; there would be no trouble or dispute about school rate-bills; there would be no difficulty in getting good teachers; the character and efficiency of the schools would be as much improved as the attendance of pupils would be increased; every child would be educated, and educated by the contribution of every man according to his means.

3. This is also the most effectual method of providing the best, as well as the cheapest, school for the youth of each school section.

Our schools are now often poor and feeble, because a large portion of the best educated inhabitants stand aloof from them, as unworhy of their support, as unfit to educate their children. Thus the Common Schools are frequently left to the care and support of the least instructed part of the population, and are then complained of as inferior in character and badly supported. The Free School system makes every man a supporter of the school according to his property. All persons—and especially the more wealthy—who are thus identified with the school, will feel interested in it; they will be anxious that their contributions to the school should be as effective as possible, and that they themselves may derive all possible benefit from it. When all the inhabitants of a school section thus become concerned in the school, its character and efficiency will inevitably be advanced. The more wealthy contributors will seek to make the school fit and efficient for the English education of their own children: the Trustees will be under no fears from the disinclination or opposition of particular individuals in employing a suitable teacher and stipulating his salary: and thus is the foundation laid for a good school, adapted to all the youth of the section. The character of the school will be as much advanced as the expense of it to individual parents will be diminished; the son of the poor man, equally with the son of the rich man, will drink from the stream of knowledge at the common fountain, and will experience corresponding elevation of thought, sentiment, feeling and pursuit. Such a sight cannot fail to gladden the heart of Christian humanity.

4. The Free School system is the true, and, I think, only effectual remedy for the pernicious and pauperising system which is at present incident to our Common Schools. Many children are now kept from school on the alleged grounds of parental poverty. How far this excuse is well founded, is immaterial to the question in hand; of the fact of the excuse itself, and of its wide-spread, blasting influence, there can be no doubt. Now, while one class of poor children are altogether deprived of the benefits of all education by parental pride or indifference, the other class of them are educated as paupers or as ragged scholars. Is it not likely that children educated under this character will imbibe the spirit of it? If we would wish them to feel and act, and rely upon themselves as freemen when they grow up to manhood, let them be educated in that spirit when young. Such is the spirit of the Free School system. It banishes the very idea of pauperism from the school. No child comes there by sufferance, but every one comes there upon the ground of right. The poor man as well as the rich man pays for the support of the school according to his means; and the right of his son to the school is thus as legal as that of the rich man's son. It is true, the poor man does not pay as large a tax in the

58

abstract as his rich neighbour, but that does not the less entitle him to the protection of the law, nor should it less entitle him to the advantages provided by law for the education of his children. The grovelling and slavish spirit of pauperism becomes extinct in the atmosphere of the Free School. Pauperism and poor laws are unknown in Free School countries; and a system of Free Schools would, in less than half a century, supersede their necessity in any country.

5. The system of Free Schools makes the best provision and furnishes the strongest inducements for the education of every youth in each school section of the land. Every parent feels that having paid his school-rate—whether little or much,—he has paid what the law requires for that year's Common School education of all his children, and that they are all entitled by law to the benefits of the school. However poor a man may be, having paid what the law requires, he can claim the education of all his children as a legal right, and not supplicate it as a cringing beggar. His children go to school, not in the character and spirit of ragged pauperism, but in the ennobling spirit of conscious right, and on equal vantage ground with others. Each parent, feeling that he has paid for the education of his children, naturally desires that they may have the benefit of it. While, therefore, the rate-bill per pupil is a temptation to each parent to keep his children from the school, the annual school-rate upon property furnishes each parent with a corresponding inducement to send his children to school—relieving trustees at the same time from all fear and uncertainty as to the means of providing for the teacher's salary. It is not, therefore, surprising to find that wherever the Free School system has been tried in Upper Canada or elsewhere, the attendance of pupils at school has increased from fifty to three hundred per cent. The facilities thus provided for the education of each child in a school section, will leave the ignorant, careless, or unnatural parent without excuse for the educational neglect of his children. The finger of universal reproof and scorn pointed at him, will soon prove more powerful than statute law, and without infringing any individual right will morally compel him, in connexion with higher considerations, to send his children to school. This system of " compulsory education," I wish to see every where in operation—the compulsion of provision for the universal education of children—the compulsion of their universal right to be educated—the compulsion of universal interest in the school—the compulsion of universal concentrated opinion in behalf of the education of every child in the land. Under such a system, in the course of ten years, an uneducated Canadian youth would be a monstrous phenomenon.

6. I think the system of Free Schools is, furthermore, most consonant with the true principles and ends of civil government.

Can a more noble and economical provision be made for the security of life, liberty and property, than the removing and preventing the accumulation of that ignorance and its attendant vices which are the great sources of insecurity and danger, and the invariable pretext, if not justification, of despotism? Are any natural rights more fundamental and sacred than those of children to such an education as will fit them for their duties as citizens? If a parent is amenable to the laws who takes away a child's life by violence, or wilfully exposes it to starvation, does he less violate the inherent rights of the child in exposing it to moral and intellectual starvation? It is noble to recognize this inalienable right of infancy and youth by providing for them the means of education to which they are entitled,—not as children of particular families, but as children of our race and country. And how perfectly does it harmonize with the true principles of civil government for every man to support the laws and all institutions designed for the common good, according to his ability. This is the acknowledged principle of all just taxation; and it is the true principle of universal education. It links every man to his fellow-man in the obligations of the common interests; it wars with that greatest, meanest foe to all social advancement—the isolation of selfish individuality; and implants and nourishes the spirit of true patriotism by making each man feel that the welfare of the whole society is his welfare—that collective interests are first in order of importance and duty, and separate interests are second. And such relations and obligations have their counterpart in the spirit and injunctions of our Divine Christianity. There, while every man is required to bear his own burden according to his ability, the strong are to aid the weak, and the rich are to supply the deficiencies of the poor. This is the pervading feature and animating spirit of the christian religion; and it is the basis of that system of supporting public schools which demands the contribution of the poor man according to his penury, and of the rich according to his abundance.

7. But against this system of Free Schools, certain objections have been made; the principal of which I will briefly answer.

First objection:—"The common schools are not fit to educate the children of the higher classes of society, and therefore these classes ought not to be taxed for the support of the common schools."

Answer.—The argument of this objection is the very cause of the evil on which the objection itself is founded. The unnatural and unpatriotic separation of the wealthier classes from the Common School has caused its inefficiency and alleged degradation. Had the wealthy classes been identified with the Common Schools equally with their poorer neighbours,—as is the case in Free School countries—the Common School would have been fit for the education of their children, and proportionally better than it now is for the education of the children of the more numerous common classes of society. In Free school cities and states, the Common Schools are acknowledged to be the best elementary Schools in such cities and states ; so much so, that the Governor of the State of Massachusetts remarked at a late school celebration, that if he had the riches of an Astor, he would send all his children through the Common School to the highest institutions in the State.

Scond objection :—" It is unjust to tax persons for the support of a school which they do not patronise, and from which they derive no individual benefit."

Answer.—If this objection be well founded, it puts an end to school taxes of every kind, and abolishes school and college endowments of every description ; it annihilates all systems of public instruction, and leaves education and schools to individual caprice and inclination. This doctrine was tried in the Belgian Netherlands after the revolt of Belgium from Holland in 1830 ; and in the course of five years, educational desolation spread throughout the kingdom, and the Legislature had to interfere to prevent the population from sinking into semi-barbarism. But the principle of a public tax for schools has been avowed in every school assessment which has ever been imposed by our Legislature, or by any District Council ; the same principle is acted upon in the endowment of a Provincial University—for such endowment is as much public property as any part of the public annual revenue of the country. The principle has been avowed and acted upon by every republican State of America, as well as by the Province of Canada and the countries of Europe. The only question is, as to the extent to which the principle should be applied—whether to raise a part or the whole of what is required to support the public school. On this point it may be remarked, that if the principle be applied at all, it should be applied in that way and to that extent which will best promote the object contemplated—namely, the sound education of the people ; and experience, as well as the nature of the case, shows, that the free system of supporting schools is the most, and indeed the only, effectual means of promoting the universal education of the people.

I observe again on this second objection, that what it assumes as fact is not true. It assumes that none are benefitted by the common school but those who patronise it. This is the lowest, narrowest and most selfish view of the subject, and indicates a mind the most contracted and grovelling. This view applied to a Provincial University, implies that no persons are benefitted by it except graduates ; applied to criminal jurisprudence and its requisite officers and prisons, it supposes that none are benefitted by them except those whose persons are rescued from the assaults of violence, or whose property is restored from the hands of theft; applied to canals, harbours, roads, &c., this view assumes that no persons derive any benefit from them except those who personally navigate or travel over them. The fact is, that whatever tends to diminish crime and lessen the expenses of criminal jurisprudence, enhances the value of the whole estate of a country or district; and is not this the tendency of good common school education? And who has not witnessed the expenditure of more money in the detection, imprisonment and punishment of a single uneducated criminal, than would be necessary to educate in the common school half a dozen children? Is it not better to spend money upon the child than upon the culprit—to prevent crime rather than punish it? Again, whatever adds to the security of property of all kinds increases its value; and does not the proper education of the people do so? Whatever also tends to develope the physical resources of a country, must add to the value of property; and is not this the tendency of the education of the people? Is not education in fact the power of the people to make all the resources of their country tributary to their interests and comforts? And is not this the most obvious and prominent distinguishing feature between an educated and uneducated people—the power of the former, and the powerlessness of the latter, to develope the resources of nature and providence, and make them subservient to human interests and enjoyments? Can this be done without increasing the value of property? I verily believe, that in the sound and universal education of the people, the balance of gain financially is on the side of the wealthier classes. If the poorer classes gain in intellectual power, and in the resources of individual and social happiness, the richer classes gain proportionally, I think more than proportionally, in the enhanced value of their property. As an illustration, take any two neighbourhoods, equal in advantages of situation and natural fertility of soil; the one inhabited by an ignorant, and therefore unenterprising, grovelling, if not disorderly, population; the other peopled with a well educated, and therefore enterprising, intelligent and industrious class of inhabitants. The difference in the value of all real estates in the two neighbourhoods is ten if not a hundred-fold greater than the amount of school-tax that has ever been imposed upon it. And yet it is the school that makes the difference in the two neighbourhoods; and the larger the field of experiment the more marked will be the difference. Hence, in free school countries, where the experiment has been so tested as to become a system, there are no warmer advocates of it than men of the largest property and the greatest intelligence; the profoundest scholars and the ablest statesmen.

It has also been objected, that the lands of absentees ought not to be taxed for the support of schools in the vicinity of such lands.

I answer, the inhabitants of the school sections in which such lands are situated, are continually adding to the value of those lands by their labours and improvements, and are therefore entitled to some return, in the shape of a local school tax, from such absentee land-holders.

The objection that the Free School system is a pauperising system has been sufficiently answered and exposed in a preceding part of this address. Such a term is only applicable to the present system, as I have shown ; and the application of it to the Free School system is an exhibition of the sheerest ignorance of the subject, or a pitiful manœuvre of selfishness against the education of the working classes of the people. History is unanimous in the assertion that the first race of New England pilgrims were the best educated and most independent class of men that ever planted the standard of colonization in any new country. Yet among these men did the system of Free Schools originate ; by their free and intelligent descendants has it been perpetuated and extended ; their universal education has triumphed over the comparative barrenness of their soil and the severity of their climate, and made their States the metropolis of American manufactures and mechanic arts, and the seat of the best colleges and schools in America. Nor is a page of their educational history disfigured with the narrative of " a Ragged School," or the anomaly of a pauper pupil.

(C) RULES OF TEACHERS' ASSOCIATIONS.

Rules of the Halifax Educational Institute.

1. This Society shall be called " The Halifax Educational Institute."

2. Its object shall be the mutual improvement of its members —the advancement of the teaching profession, and the extension of Education.

3. The mode of effecting these objects shall be : meetings for the discussion of educational subjects—the delivery ot lectures— explanation and examination of proposed improvements, and such other means as may seem desirable.

The proceedings specified in this rule shall have a practical and scientific tendency.

4. The officers shall be a President, Vice President, Secretary,

and Committee of three, whose duty shall be to manage and arrange respecting the meetings, and other affairs of the Society.

The officers shall be elected annually at the second meeting in September.

5. All teachers shall be eligible to membership. The Superintendent of Education, Commissioners and Trustees of Schools, shall be honorary members. Other honorary members may be elected by a unanimous vote at a regular meeting. Ladies engaged in teaching may be members of the Institute, by agreeing to its rules, without payment.

6. The regular meetings shall take place on Saturday, once a fortnight, commencing at 3 o'clock and closing not later than 5.

7. For defraying requisite expenses, two shillings and six pence entrance fee, and one shilling and three pence quarterly, shall be paid by each member. All monies and property of the Society shall be in charge of the Secretary. The President shall keep a duplicate record of receipts and disbursements.

8. The regular meetings shall be opened aud closed with prayer, by the President or some person provided by him.

9. The general mode of occupying the time at regular meetings shall be :

First—The delivery of an Essay.

Second—Conversation on the merits of the Essay in its elocution, grammar, rhetoric, logic and sentiments, with summing up by the chairman. Free criticism shall be considered desirable, as a valuable means of mutual improvement. A vote may be taken on any disputed point, at the discretion of the chairman.

Third—Suggestions and illustrations resulting from the essay or conversation.

Fourth—Miscellaneous business.

10. The arrangements of Rule 9 may be set aside when other educational subjects appear to demand precedence.

Rules of the Stirling Association of Teachers.

1. Agreed that the Teachers in the district of Stirling form themselves into an Association, to be denominated "The Stirling Association of Teachers."

2. That the object of this Association shall be, the mutual improvement of its members in whatever has a tendency to increase their qualifications for rendering them more competent for the discharge of their professional duties ; also the adoption of such measures as tend to facilitate the business of instruction.

3. That the Association be governed by a President, Secretary and Treasurer, to be elected annually.

4. That a chairman be chosen at each meeting for the purpose of superintending the business pro tem.

5. That a Lecture or Essay shall be delivered at each sederunt by the retiring chairman.

6. That every member shall pay one shilling and three pence entrance fee, and six pence quarterly.

7. That this Association shall have its regular meetings quarterly, and that intermediate meetings may be called for the above specified purposes.

8. That these shall be considered as the standing rules of the society, subject to additions and amendments.

Rules of Durham Teachers' Association, (Pictou county.)

1. That this Association shall be denominated the " Durham Teachers' Association."

2. The object of the members of this Association is, their mutual improvement in the practical art of teaching, in literary, mathematical, and scientific pursuits, and the advancement of the profession (so far as is in their power) to its proper position in society.

3. The office-bearers in this Association shall be a President, a Vice President, Secretary and Treasurer, and three of a Committee—to be elected annually, three of whom shall constitute a quorum for the transaction of business.

4. Any teacher, or person intending to become a teacher, shall be eligible for membership.

5. Every member of this Association shall pay seven pence half-penny entrance fee, and three pence quarterly.

Bye-Laws.

1. The members of this Association shall be on a footing of equality in every respect, eligible to all offices, and liable to perform all duties required for the advancement of the interests of the Association.

2. It shall be the duty of every member to correct any ungrammatical expression, either in spoken or written composition, inaccurate pronunciation, &c.,—all to be done in a fair and candid spirit of criticism.

3. The members of this Association shall visit each others schools twice in each year, if practicable.

4. The Committee shall appoint a member to lecture at each meeting of the Association.

5. Any member who shall neglect to perform his duty, shall be fined 7½d. for the first, and 1s. 3d. each for every succeeding default, unless excused by the Association.

6. The meetings of this Association shall be open to the public at all times.

7. The meetings of this Association shall be held in the Durham school house every alternate Saturday, at 3 o'clock. p. m.

8. No alteration or amendment shall be made in these rules except at a regular semi-annual meeting; however, any bye-law may be suspended by a unanimous vote.

Rules of Sydney Teachers' Association.

1. That licensed Teachers only shall be admitted members of this Association.

2. That every member shall pay a fee of one shilling and three pence annually.

3. That the members of this Association shall meet on the first Saturday of every month, at 12 o'clock, noon.

4. That the Association shall at each meeting appoint a Chairman to preside over it for next month; that the Secretary shall be appointed for three months; and that the Treasurer shall be elected annually.

5. That a Committee chosen by the Association shall visit the schools of members and report to the Association.

Besides the above, it was agreed, that, at next meeting, a code of bye-laws for the special regulation of the Association, should be adopted, and that steps should be taken to institute a Library and Museum for the special benefit of Teachers in connection with the Association.

(D.) NOTES OF THE PROCEEDINGS OF THE INSTITUTE HELD AT TRURO, NOVEMBER, 1851.

The following notes can make no pretension to give a full or orderly account of the proceedings of the Institute :—They consist of a selection of views which appeared to meet with general approval, and which it is supposed may be useful to teachers. In compiling them, the superintendent has been assisted by Mr. Farquhar, of Musquodoboit, Miss Gauld, of Maitland, and Mr. Cutten, of Amherst, who kindly favored him with extracts from their note-books.

The order of exercises for each day was as follows : Meeting at 9; a. m., for opening address, and review of past day's proceedings; 11, a. m., recess, during which the experiments for the lecture on Agricultural chemistry were prepared, and questions asked on that subject; 12, lecture on Agricultural chemistry, by the Superintendent; 1, p. m., recess; 2, p. m., meeting for discussions and illustrations; 7, p. m., lectures, &c.

At the close of the meeting, an address was presented to the Superintendent, and resolutions were passed approving of a Normal School, and of Free Schools supported by assessment, and recommending the establishment of associations of teachers.

On Monday, the educational meeting for the district was held in the morning, and the Superintendent lectured in the evening.

On Tuesday, the institute having been opened by prayer, was addressed by the Superintendent, on the nature and utility of such meetings, and the rules for conducting them, and inviting a free discussion of the suggestions which might be made; after which the institute proceeded to discuss the subject of

ENGLISH READING AND SPELLING.

on which the following views seemed to be generally approved:—

The initiatory lessons in English reading are of especial importance, since, if these be properly given, the future progress of the pupil is comparatively easy.

One of two methods may be followed: 1st—the mechanical; 2d—the intellectual and mechanical combined.

In the first, the pupil, having learned the alphabet, proceeds to syllables, and thence to words, arranged according to their number of syllables, &c., without at first making reading a branch of intellectual culture. This method assumes that the alphabet really contains the elements of the sounds of the language. Since, however, our alphabet is not phonetic, but very variable and arbitrary in the sounds of its letters when combined in words, this method must be tedious and repulsive to the learners.

The second method bases its instructions on the ideas of the learner. It takes some simple word, whose meaning is known to the child, shows the word in a book, finds out its letters, and thus teaches the alphabet by degrees, and in connection with the meaning of words, and of easy sentences. This method is in most cases easy, useful and pleasant: it cultivates the thinking powers, and shows the use of reading.

On no account allow the pupil to resume his seat, without knowing something of the meaning of the words he has read.

Teach the letters by their sounds rather than their names. Thus instead of see-ay-tee, which are not the sounds of the letters of the word cat, we say *ik-a-it*, the *i* being only a *breathing*.

Letters on cards are useful, and the learners should have words printed on the blackboard to copy on their slates.

Class teaching at the blackboard is also very useful, especially when the pupils are not provided with uniform books.

Separate spelling lessons are useless to young scholars. They should be required to spell the words of the reading lesson. *Advanced* scholars may, if necessary, have spelling lessons containing difficult words.

It is unnecessary to spend time in reading syllables, or dividing words into syllables. The latter art is useful in dividing words at the end of the line in writing; but to divide according to the sound, (and composition in the case of compound words,) is the best rule for this.

The use of spelling is to enable us to *write* words correctly. Written spelling on slate and paper should therefore be commenced as early as possible, and should be the *principal* spelling lesson. Oral spelling may be by letters, words and sentences, individually and simultaneously : all are useful and should be often varied.

Pupils should be taught to define words by a full explanation of the meaning, or by giving an example of their use.

Reading lessons should not be too long to prevent full examination on their meaning.

It is useful to question pupils before they begin to read, respecting the subject of the lesson, &c.

Reading is learned that we may obtain knowledge and mental improvement. These ends should therefore be kept in view in the school lessons, and the pupil should be trained to think as he reads. The habit of reading without attending, once acquired can rarely be entirely overcome, while on the other hand a skilful teacher can give an invaluable mental training, by means of the school lessons.

The teacher should read to the class a part of every lesson.

Simultaneous reading, as an *occasional* exercise, has been found useful in advancing the more backward pupils.

Monotonous, singing, drawling, too loud and too low reading, should be corrected *from the first*. It will be found that such habits often proceed from neglect of the meaning of the passage read. It is sometimes useful to require different pupils to read the same sentence, till they succeed in doing it correctly.

Advanced classes should be required to give written and oral abstracts or paraphrases of passages read, and such lessons should be made to afford instruction at once in spelling, grammar and composition.

The teacher should study the reading lesson before the class read it.

Every reading lesson should, if possible, be made to extend the learner's knowledge of the *uses* of English words.

68

The readers should be at their ease, and encouraged to have confidence. If *afraid* of the teacher, he cannot teach them to read *well*.

Elocution is usually viewed as an advanced department of reading, but very young pupils may be trained to use proper inflexion and emphasis, if they understand what they read. On the other hand, it is impossible to read well either in respect to inflexion or emphasis, unless the reader comprehends and enters into the sense of the matter read.

The subject of phonotypy or phonetic reading, is well worthy the attention of teachers; more especially as it has been found to be a rapid and easy means of introducing pupils into the ordinary reading.

On Tuesday, at 12 o'clock, the Superintendent lectured on Agricultural Chemistry; and in the evening, after a musical performance conducted by ladies and gentlemen of Truro, he lectured on the introduction of music and drawing into schools—the cultivation of taste in the pupils—improvement of school houses and play grounds, and other allied subjects.

On Wednesday, after review of some of the topics of the past day, the Institute entered on the subject of

ENGLISH GRAMMAR.

After some remarks by the Superintendent, the discussion was opened by several teachers who had attended the Institute held at Pictou, and who now stated their experience in the practice of the method recommended there of commencing the study of Grammar by oral exercises, with the aid of the blackboard, before requiring any part of a text book to be studied or committed to memory.

On the subject of oral lessons in grammar, it was remarked:

1. Very young children may be taught grammar, because they all have, even before they enter school, a practical grammar of their own.

2. Grammar *should* be taught to young children, because otherwise they may be daily acquiring and strengthening habits of speaking incorrectly.

3. These oral lessons should be founded on the child's previous stock of knowledge, and he should be first taught to arrange the words he knows, in classes or separate parts of speech. Thus the teacher may say, holding up a book—"What is this?"—(A book.) "The word you have said is"—(the name of it.) "When we speak or write we must have—(names) for the things we speak or write about," &c. The word "book" may then be written on the black-

board, and the pupils may be required to give other words which are the names of things; correcting and explaining when they are wrong. The pupils may then be told that words of this kind are called in grammar, nouns. From nouns, the teacher may in the same manner go on to the adjective, article, and pronoun—verb, adverb, conjunction, preposition and interjection, which will be found a better arrangment than that in most grammars.

4. In the first course of oral lessons the learner should not be troubled with such difficulties as the formation of plurals or the inflexions of the verb. These should be reserved for a second course, which may be given with the aid of the book.

5. In oral lessons to young scholars, very simple explanations should be given, as "nouns are the names of the things, persons and places we speak of"—"adjectives tell the kinds of things"—"verbs shew what the things are, what they do, and what is done to them," &c.; and these simple definitions should be varied as much as possible.

6. The teacher should have several good books of grammar, to which he may refer for definitions and simple explanations.

7. After teaching the parts of speech, the simpler rules of syntax may be taught orally—or, if the class be not very young, they may study syntax from the book at once.

8. All ungrammatical expressions should be corrected on the instant. This *practical* teaching of grammar is of great importance.

9. It is very useful to point out to children that the division of parts of speech is not arbitrary; that is, that in order to express our thoughts, we must have several different kinds of words, which have, so to speak, different trades and occupations. In like manner it should also be pointed out that most of the ways of using words which are considered to be correct, or in other words most of the rules of syntax, are founded on common sense.

10. The teacher should beware of overlooking the simpler parts of his subject, or of leading his pupils beyond their depth.

On the subject of advanced lessons with the aid of the book, the importance of full explanations, and of questions as to uses and reasons was insisted on.

It was also recommended that written exercises should be given as often as possible. These may be either elliptical lessons, in which the scholar must supply the deficient words, topics or incidents on which he must write, or abstracts of passages in reading books. Such lessons are at once useful in teaching spelling, writing, grammar and composition.

While, in the introductory oral lessons, hard words should be avoided as much as possible, in the advanced course, the pupil should learn the technical terms, and the teacher should endeavour to make the grammar lessons the means of extending the pupil's command of words and power of expressing himself.

The teacher should cultivate correct habits of speaking, and endeavour to overcome any inaccurate forms of expression into which he may have fallen.

At the close of the discussion on grammar, Mr. Yewens, of Shubenacadie, gave illustrations, with a class formed of teachers, of the method of teaching grammar orally, as practised in one of the Normal Schools of England.

On Wednesday evening, Mr. Robertson, one of the teachers, addressed the Institute on some of the difficulties of the teacher's position; after which, Mr. Blanchard, of the Truro Academy, gave explanations of the rules of Elocution, with examples, and the Superintendent performed experiments illustrative of the chemical lecture of the forenoon.

On Thursday the subject of

ARITHMETIC

occupied the greater part of the day, and a number of illustrations of particular rules were given, which it would be impossible to repeat here.

It was recommended to begin with oral instructions, accompanied by copying figures on the slate.

The oral notation from one to ten, and then by "teens" and "ties," should be explained, followed by easy lessons in mental calculation, with the aid of Colburn or some other good book. Mental arithmetic may be taught to very young scholars, and will be a useful relief from the monotony of constant reading lessons.

The counting frame or arithmeticon, will be found very useful, as well as measures of length, capacity, &c., drawn in their natural proportions, on the walls of the school room.

In mental arithmetic, the pupils should be required to explain the process by which they have obtained the answer.

In slate arithmetic, the importance of a thorough grounding in numeration was strongly insisted on.

The teaching should be in classes as much as possible, and the class may either write on slates, or one by one, state the process as the teacher writes it on the black board. These methods, when skilfully pursued, cause much animation and rapid progress.

Every rule should be thoroughly explained by examples on the black board, before the pupils are allowed to work questions alone.

Arithmetic usually requires frequent repetition and review.

The teacher should carefully study the principles on which the rules are founded, and for this purpose should have a variety of good books. The advanced arithmetic of Chambers' course, and Thomson's arithmetic, were especially recommended as useful in this way.

It is not necessary to teach the tables of moneys, measures, &c., till they are required in the compound rules.

The compound rules should be taught on the same principle as ordinary numeration ; with the explanation that here the gradation of increased value is often irregular, instead of by tens. Thus we carry 12 pence to the shillings place as 1 shilling, on precisely the same principle with carrying 10 units to the place of tens as 1 ten. The money of the United States furnishes an illustration of a table identical with the common numeration : thus 1 eagle, 1 dollar. 1 dime, 1 cent, 1 mill, are equal to 11,111 mills.

On Thursday evening, Mr. H. Oldright of Halifax, lectured on Phonetic spelling. He pointed out the absurdities and difficulties of the present orthography, and the ease and rapidity with which reading might be taught by the use of a phonetic alphabet. He also explained the nature of phonographic writing, and on the following day gave a class illustration of the method of acquiring and teaching it. Previous to the commencement of the lecture, an illustration of drawing on the black board was given by the superintendent.

On Friday the attention of the institute was directed to the subject of

SCHOOL DISCIPLINE AND ORDER.

In this we should have first the heart education or moral training of the pupils, and secondly the promotion of the progress of the school. The means employed for the latter should always be consistent with the former.

Kind, quiet and firm government mark a superior teacher, and where harsh measures must be frequently resorted to, or continual clamouring for order is maintained, it is to be inferred that the teacher's personal influence is small. Above all, the teacher must regulate his own temper if he would maintain order.

The teacher must present to his pupils an example of punctuality, order, patience and industry. An idle or careless teacher must always have a bad school.

The teacher should study the various tempers of his pupils, as well as their degrees of intellectual powers.

He should avoid threatening, and have few absolute rules. The rules which are prescribed must be strictly enforced. . Absolute obedience must be insisted on.

Corporal punishment should be one of the last resources, and should be administered in private, and the culprit should, if possible, be made to see and regret the evil of his conduct. Corporal punishment should be inflicted only for disobedience or grave moral offences.

Young children on their first coming to school, should be allowed for a day or two to accustom themselves to their new circumstances, before discipline is regularly enforced on them.

It was recommended to teachers to keep a note book of offences during school hours, and to deal with the offenders at recess, or at the close of the school.

The system of registering errors and merits was strongly recommended by teachers who had tried it. It saves time, instead of wasting it as some apprehend, and has a powerful influence on the pupils.

Trapping, or taking places in classes, should be abandoned if found to produce envy or unwholsome emulation.

The virtues of self-denial, perseverance, punctuality, industry, honesty and truthfulness should be cultivated in every practicable manner, and no opportunity of insisting on their importance should be allowed to pass unimproved.

When prizes are given, they should be distributed according to the register of conduct and recitation for the previous half year, or by a vote of the class.

The teacher should take cognizance of the conduct of pupils in the play ground, and in coming to and returning from school, but not beyond this.

Pupils who fail in completing their lessons without good excuse, should be kept in after hours.

It is not proper to notice very trifling offences. These had better be passed by.

The teacher will find it in the highest degree conducive to his own comfort and usefulness to study carefully the subject of school discipline, and to cultivate by means of it the highest moral feelings of his pupils.

———

On Friday evening a Soiree was held in the Temperance Hall, at which a number of interesting speeches on educational subjects were delivered by the teachers and others.

———

On Saturday, the Superintendent summed up the views of the Institute on the subjects discussed, adding some remarks on the teaching of Geography; after which, Charles Blanchard, Esq. was called to the chair, and the teachers proceeded to present the address and pass the resolutions already mentioned.

(E) FORMS OF REGISTERS OF ERRORS AND MERITS.

I.   CLASS REGISTER OF ERRORS AND MERITS.

Mathematical class from 2 to 3 o'clock.	Week commencing Sept. 9, 1850.					Aver-age.	Week commencing Sept. 16.					Aver-age.
R. M ——	8	8	8	8	8	8						
C. G. ——	7	6	✠	✠	✠	6½						
D. M ——	5	✠	7	6	7	6 1-5						
J. R. ——	6	7	7	6	—							
L. P. ——	7	7	7	+	8	7 1-5						
D. F. ——	7	7	7	7	8	7 1 5						
G. C. ——	7	8	8	8	8	7 4 5						
W.C. ——	8	5	7	8	7	7						
J. C. ——	6	0	0	5	7	3 3-5						
W.M. ——	6	4	5	7	7	5 4-5						

The above is a Class Register, on the plan of the Irish National Schools. It is copied from the Register of a Class in the Pictou Academy, and includes only five days ; Saturday being devoted to review, and marked in another place.

8 is the highest merit ; 1 the lowest ; 0 is equivalent to not at all prepared. As the class exercise goes on, or after it is over, the teacher marks on a slate the number of errors committed, and from this, with allowance for unusual difficulties, &c., fixes the mark for that day. The weekly average is, of course, the sum of the days divided by 5.

Absences are marked (✠), or (—). If absent without excuse, (—) ; if absent with a note from the parent (✠). If without excuse, the average is obtained by dividing by the whole number of days. If there be a good excuse, the days for which there is an excuse are subtracted from the divisor. Thus C. G. was absent three days ; but having an excuse, his numbers for the remaining two days are divided by 2. If he had brought no excuse, these numbers would have been divided by 5, leaving his average 3 1-5 instead of 6½. J. R. has a *minus* mark, but his average is left blank to give him an opportunity to bring an excuse.

The Register of Conduct is kept in the same manner. The ordinary Register of the School may easily be made a Conduct Register, in the following manner. When the roll is called in the morning, mark all absentees with a *minus*, and leave the space opposite those present blank. During the day, note all misdemeanors on a slate, or employ a monitor to do so. Then, at the close of the day, mark all the well-behaved 8, and others with lower numbers in proportion to their conduct. Those who are too late are marked as delinquents, if they have no excuse. If they bring an excuse, they are counted as present, Those marked (—) for absence, are left so, unless they bring an excuse on the following day.

In obtaining the *average attendance* of the school, all the numbers are added as units. In obtaining the *average conduct* of the pupil, they are added according to their value, and divided by the number of days, after deducting excused absence. The following is an example:

II. REGISTER OF CONDUCT AND ATTENDANCE.

	M	T	W	T	F	S	Av'ge.	Remarks.
G. R.——	8	8	*2	8	‡	‡	6 1-2	* Quarreling.
J. R.——	8	8	8	8	8	8	8	†Whispering in ⎱
P. F.——	8	8	8	‡	8	8	8	study hours. ⎰
T. K.——	8	†7	†7	8	8	8	7 2-3	‡ Too late.
A. C.——	4	8	8	8	8	8	7 1-3	
W.P.——	8	8	8	‡	‡	8	8	
R. M.——	‡	8	8	‡6	8	8	7 3 5	
Attendance,	6	7	7	5	5	6	6	

The following is a form of *Weekly Report* to the parents or guardians. Such reports are usually intended to pass between the parent and teacher, for a quarter or a term. In the form below, only a few weeks have been given, merely as a specimen. A Monthly Report may, of course, be made out in the same manner, in cases where the teacher has not time to attend to a Weekly Report, or finds that the parents will not attend to it. Where Weekly Reports are used, the forms should be printed to save trouble.

WEEKLY REPORT OF THE CONDUCT OF C. D—— FROM —— TO ——.

DATE.	Attendance	Conduct.	Reading.	Arithmetic	Grammar.	Geography.		Name of parent.
November 9,	6	8	5	7 2-5	7 1-5	6½		T. D——
16,	4	8	6 2-5	8	7 3.5	5 2-5		T. D——
23,	5	7	7	6	5 1.5	8		T. D——
30,	6	6½	8	8	7 1-5	8		T. D——
December 7,	5½	7⅔	7 2-5	8	8	6⅔		

The card is sent home at the end of every week, and the parent signs his name or initials in the last column, and returns it to the teacher on Monday.

(F)   LIST OF BOOKS

RECOMMENDED FOR USE IN SCHOOLS, BY THE SUPERINTENDENT OF EDUCATION.

Those marked thus (*) are especially recommended as Text Books.

I. ENGLISH READING.

(A) ELEMENTARY BOOKS FOR YOUNGER CLASSES.

*CHAMBERS's FIRST BOOK OF READING.—Adapted to the intelligence of Children under six years of age,   price   2d

*CHAMBERS's SECOND BOOK OF READING—A Regular Series of Lessons on the Consonants, for more advanced pupils,   price   4d

*CHAMBERS's SIMPLE LESSONS IN READING—Calculated to advance the learner in Reading and Spelling.   price   1 0½d

*CHAMBERS's RUDIMENTS OF KNOWLEDGE —In this work the child is introduced in a progressive manner, and by lessons to be read in schools, to a knowledge of the external appearances in the natural and social world ; the explanations being given in simple language, suitable to juvenile minds.   price   1 0½d

CHAMBERS's MORAL CLASS BOOK.—In a series of advanced Reading Lessons this volume describes the more important Moral and Economic Duties of Life, illustrating them by means of Anecdotes, Historical and Biographical, by Fables and other Narratives, together with a selection of Scriptural Passages and Apothegms.   price 1   10½d

*THIRD LESSONS, or Spelling Book of the Scottish Association Series. [White & Co., Edinburgh.]   7½d

The First, Second, Fourth and Fifth Books of the Association Series are also very excellent, being a highly successful attempt to combine the classification of sounds and words with interesting lessons. The elementary works of *McCulloch's, the Irish National*, and *Leitch's* Series, are also very good, and may be combined with Chambers's, when desired.

(B) BOOKS FOR ADVANCED CLASSES.

	s.	d.
*Chambers's History of the British Empire,	3	1½
*Chambers's Elocution,	3	1½
————— English Language and Literature,	3	1½
————— Exemplary and Instructive Biography,	3	1½
*————— Introduction to the Sciences,	1	3
————— Matter and Motion,	1	0½
————— Mechanics,	1	0½
————— Hydrostatics,	1	0½
————— Astronomy,	1	3
————— Electricity,	1	3
————— Meteorology,	1	3
*————— Animal Physiology.	1	10½
————— History of Rome,	3	1½
————— History of Greece,	3	1½
*————— Ancient History,	3	9

	s.	d.
McCulloch's Course of Reading,	3	9
Parker's First Lessons in Natural Philosophy,	2	0
Parker's Compendium of Natural Philosophy,	5	0
Blake's Natural Philosophy,	3	6
Cutter's First Book of Physiology,	2	6
———— Treatise on Anatomy and Physiology,	5	9
The Holy Scriptures.		

II. ARITHMETIC AND BOOK-KEEPING.

	s.	d.
* Chambers's Introduction to Arithmetic,	1	3
" Advanced Treatise on ditto,	2	6
Thomson's Arithmetic, (Irish National series,)	2	8
* Colburn's Intellectual Arithmetic.	1	0
* Wilcolke's & Fryer's Mental Arithmetic, edited by Rev. J. Waddell,		
* Selden's Mental Arithmetic,	0	7½
* Chambers's Book-keeping,	2	6
Hutton's do. (Imp. by Ingram,)	2	6
Morrison's Book-keeping.		

III. GRAMMAR AND COMPOSITION.

	s.	d.
* Lennie's English Grammar,	1	0
* Chambers's Introduction to Grammar,	1	7
* " Advanced Grammar, two parts, each	1	10½
* " Introduction to Composition,	0	7½
Reid's Rudiments of English Composition,	2	6
* Chambers's Etymology,	2	6
Wood's Etymological Guide, (Sessional school,)	3	1½
Lynd's First Book of Etymology,	2	0
* McCulloch's Prefixes and Affixes,	0	2

IV. GEOGRAPHY.

	s.	d.
* Chambers's Geographical Primer,	0	10
* Morse's Quarto Geography,	2	6
* Stewart's Modern Geography,	4	4½
Handbook of the Geography of Nova Scotia	1	3
Chambers's Primer Atlas,	3	1½
" School Atlas,	13	1½
Fowle's Outline Maps, (8 Maps, 27 ins. x 27.)	20	0
Mitchell's Revised Series of Outline Maps, (15 Maps,)	40	0
" Hemispheres, with book,	7	6
Chambers's Hemispheres, (5 feet 2 ins. x 4 feet 6 ins.)	26	3
Dawson's Map of Nova Scotia, (22 ins. x 24, new ed. in press)	2	6
Cornell's Patent 5-inch Globe,	15	0

V. ALGEBRA AND MATHEMATICS.

	s.	d.
*Bell's Algebra, (Chambers's Course),	4	4½
Sherwin's Elementary Algebra,	5	0
*Plane Geometry, first six books of Euclid, (Chambers's Course),	3	1½
*Solid and Spherical Geometry, and Conic Sections, do,	3	1½
*Bell's Practical Mathematics, ditto, 2 parts, (and Tables,) each,	5	0
Davies' Algebra ; Monro's Surveying.		

VI. AGRICULTURAL CHEMISTRY.

*Johnston's Catechism of Agricultural Chemistry,	9d. to 1s. 3d.
Norton's Elements of Scientific Agriculture,	1s. 3d. to 3s. 9d.
Johnston's Elements of Agricultural Chemistry,	2s. 6d.
Johnston's Lectures do.	7s. 6d.

VII. DIRECTORIES FOR TEACHERS.

The School and School Master, by Potter & Emerson, (Harper, New York,)	$1 0
The Teacher's Manual, by Palmer, Boston : Marsh, Capen & Co.	0 75 cts.
Theory and Practice of Teaching, by Page, New York,	1 0
Mann's Lectures on Education. Boston . Fowle & Capen,	1 0
Wood's Account of the Edinburgh Sessional School, (Edinburgh),	6s. 3d.
Journal of Education of Upper Canada, (Toronto, Monthly,)	5s pr ann.
The Massachusetts Teacher, (Boston, Monthly.)	
Alcott's Slate and Blackboard Exercises, (New York, Newman,)	37 cts.
Chambers's Infant Education, from two to six years,	2s 6d
Barnard's School Architecture. Barnes : New York.	
Ryerson's Report on a system of Public Elementary Instruction for Upper Canada. Montreal, 1847.	
The Blackboard in the Primary School—(Boston)	

(G) APPENDIX TO STATISTICAL TABLES.

Expenditure of the sum of £600, appropriated to the purchase of School Books and Apparatus, and of the balance of the grant for Institutes.

City of Halifax, (paid Comm'rs. £35, Books 45s.)		£37	5	0
Eastern Halifax,	School Books,	19	17	0
Western Halifax,	do,	19	17	0
Lunenburg,	do,	34	16	0
Queen's County,	do,	19	17	0
Annapolis,	do,	32	10	0
King's County,	do,	32	7	0
Northern Pictou,	do,	31	6	0
Southern Pictou,	do,	31	8	0
Parrsboro',	do,	5	12	6
Cumberland,	do,	25	0	0
Colchester,	do,	23	17	4½
Stirling,	do,	9	14	0
Eastern Hants,	do,	13	14	6
Western Hants,	do,	19	17	0
Clare,	do,	8	19	3
Digby,	do,	18	10	0
Yarmouth,	do,	16	17	0
Argyle,	do,	11	0	6
Barrington,	do,	10	0	0
Shelburne,	do,	10	0	0
St. Mary's,	do,	9	10	0
Guysborough,	do,	19	0	0
Sydney,	do,	33	0	0
Southern Inverness,	do,	28	0	0
Northern Inverness,	do,	17	0	0
Cape Breton,	do,	22	14	0
Victoria,	do,	22	14	0
Richmond,	do,	24	15	0
Printing Journal of Education, Returns, &c.,		26	18	0
Expenses of forwarding parcels, Canadian Journal to Associations, duties, cases, advertising Institutes, &c.,		15	11	2
Balance in hands of Superintendent,		0	4	11
		£651	12	2½

CR.

By balance from 1850,	£0	0	5	
" Grant for Books, &c.,	600	0	0	
" Balance of Institute Grant,	36	4	5	
" Additional discounts on Books,	15	7	4½	
				£651 12 2½

NOTE.—In the above account, deductions have been made from the amounts charged in the bills of several districts, on account of Maps of Nova Scotia, charged in the bills, but which could not be procured in time to be forwarded with the other parcels.

———

ABSTRACT OF RETURN OF TRURO ACADEMY, HALF YEAR ENDING NOVEMBER 1, 1851.

Teachers.—Jonathan Blanchard, head master ; William H. Clow, assistant.

Number of paid pupils, 81 ; free pupils, 5.

Support from people, £50 7s. 4d. ; from province, £50.

Number of pupils in Latin, 11 ; in French, 9 ; in Mathematics, 13 ; in Agricultural Chemistry, 7.

CPSIA information can be obtained
at www.ICGtesting.com
Printed in the USA
BVHW091240101218
535227BV00012B/513/P